ANTIQUE AUTOMOBILES

ANTIQUE AUTOMOBILES

by Anthony Bird

TREASURE PRESS

JAMES' STEAM COACH, 1829

This rather imaginative representation of William James' third steam coach was designed to attract subscribers to the company formed by James' backer, Sir James Anderson. Lack of capital prevented the development of James' vehicles: also metallurgical science was not advanced enough to cope with the very high pressures for which he designed his water-tube boilers. Next page: Fuel problem as seen by cartoonist in 1827.

There are still people to be found who say they wish the motor car had never been invented; more particularly they wish the internal combustion engine had never been thought of as then, they say, there would have been no aeroplanes either. Looking at our choked and over-crowded streets, sickened by the filthy fumes from diesel engines and deafened by the din of jet-planes one is sometimes tempted to agree with them, but from the moment when man first used a piece of stick or a stone to supplement his fingers it was inevitable that one day he would make a wheel, and then a carriage, and then a horse-less carriage and all the rest. Setting prejudice aside one must agree that the transport revolution of the past 150 years (of which the motor car is but one aspect) has done much more good than harm.

It is strange but undeniable that methods of transportation lagged behind other developments; the sophisticated man of the eighteenth century, for example, in effect stepped back several centuries in time when he left his elegant and beautifully proportioned house, with its fine furniture, paintings, porcelain, clocks and books, to go a-travelling. We cannot trace the exact chronology of events with any certainty: when did man first put a plank underneath a load to make a primitive sledge? When did he discover that saplings or branches could be used as

STEVIN'S SAILING WAGGON 1599

It was built by the mathematician Simon Stevin for the Statholder of the Netherlands and was said to have carried 28 people for 42 miles in two hours. It is difficult to see how this could have been done, unless most of the people were very very tiny but it was probably the first land vehicle to move without the aid of human or animal power.

rollers to make the task easier? How long did it take him to cut slices from a huge fallen tree, mount them upon a length of smaller tree-trunk and so furnish himself with a pair of wheels and an axle? We do not know the exact sequence of these happenings, for they belong to pre-history, but in historical times we can trace a great leap forward under the Roman Empire followed by stagnation for several centuries.

The wheeled vehicles, such as they were, of pre-Christian times can only have been of very limited use, because without roads carriages or carts are too easily upset or stuck in the mud to be of much use. There certainly must have been roads of some sort (probably a form of tram-road of masonry blocks) along which to haul the massive stones for the Pyramids; the tribes of northern Germany (as we now know it) at a very early period made log-tracks very similar to the 'corduroy' roads still found in remote areas of the modern world, and even the supposedly primitive Ancient Britons had developed the use of the war chariot to a surprising extent before the Roman conquest; but although war chariots and wheeled carts or trolleys for dealing with difficult loads existed in times of remote antiquity, the wheeled vehicle could not come into its own until there were decent roads to use it on.

It is a commonplace of history that the Romans were the first great road builders; indeed the Empire was held together by its roads, and at the height of the Roman glory the imperial couriers, using relays of fast horses, could traverse Europe at speeds which were not equalled, let alone excelled, for some eight hundred years after the Empire declined. For the sad thing is that as the Empire crumbled so did the roads; as they were primarily military it was nobody's business to keep them in order once the military power of Rome waned and anarchy took its place. Even when the Roman roads were at their best one would have seen few wheeled vehicles upon them. Well-engineered though the high-ways were, their surfaces must have been very rough by our standards, and as the principle of flexible suspension, or springing, had not been discovered, goods waggons had to be made uneconomically massive and heavy to withstand the pounding, whilst for those who could not ride on horseback some kind of litter or carrying-chair provided a less uncomfortable ride than a wheeled carriage.

As the Roman roads disappeared beneath the turf travellers had to

PITY THE POOR FOOTMAN
An eighteenth century design for a pedal-propelled carriage.

8

be content with walking if they could not afford to ride, and goods too heavy for a man's back went by pack-animal. Broadly speaking this state of affairs persisted for several centuries and the growth of trade and commerce between countries is a tribute to man's persistence in the face of almost insuperable difficulties. Exceptionally large or heavy loads, cannon for instance, could not be carried and had to be put on wheels, but the great number of horses or oxen needed to drag heavy loads kept the wheeled cart at an economic disadvantage.

Passenger carriages began to appear in Western Europe at the beginning of the twelfth century, but they were exclusive to Royalty or to ladies of high birth who were too delicate to ride, and even they generally preferred the horse-litter for long journeys as the hooded, springless carts, however sumptuously decorated, must have been hideously uncomfortable once they left the few hundred yards of paved street to be found in the principal cities. From the twelfth to the sixteenth centuries these passenger carriages were scarcely to be found outside central and western Europe, and the first coach known to have been built in England was made for the Earl of Rutland in 1555. The first English State Coach was commissioned by Queen Elizabeth in 1571.

If England had been slow to start she soon caught up with Europe, and stage waggons, carrying a few passengers as well as goods, were operating fairly regularly by the end of Elizabeth's reign; in summer time they were able to cover about twenty miles a day. A great step forward came in about 1665 when a Colonel Blount, and one or two other innovators, began to suspend coach bodies on steel springs. Hitherto the only attempt at flexible suspension, gradually adopted during the first half of the seventeenth century, had been to hang the coach body on leather straps attached to posts rising up from the four corners of the underframing: the two posts at the back were attached to the back axle-tree, and the front posts were fastened to the massive central beam, called the 'perch' which tied the fore-carriage to the back axle-tree. This form of suspension mitigated the discomfort a little and substituted for the jolts a rocking, swaying motion very trying to those with weak stomachs, but as soon as flexible steel springs were used to supplement or supplant the straps it was possible to make the carriages much lighter as well as more comfortable. Goods waggons or carts were not

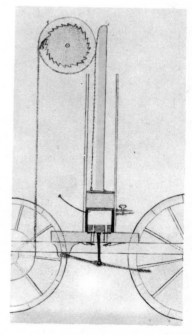

RIVAZ'S 'EXPLOSION ENGINE'
The 'explosion engine' of Rivaz's experimental vehicle.

spring-mounted until the nineteenth century, but passenger coaches immediately benefitted from the new invention and their increased usefulness stimulated demand for better roads. The spring-mounted vehicles, being lighter, were less liable to breakdown and with less expenditure of horse-power they could travel further in a given time than their predecessors. By the early eighteenth century a service of 'Flying Machines' (i.e. steel sprung stage coaches) was proudly advertised to operate between London and York at the hair-raising average speed — in Summer only, God and Weather permitting — of four miles an hour.

This says all that needs to be said of early eighteenth century roads, and it certainly seems odd that an age which had seen the solution to so many problems, and the birth of the scientific era, could put up with such primitive means of travel. The contrast between the beautiful precision timekeepers evolved by men of the calibre of Tompion, Graham or Knibb, and the advanced engineering and metallurgical techniques needed to produce them, with the lumbering stage-waggons hauled by teams of straining horses over roads which were little better than quagmires for much of the year is ludicrous indeed. The improvement throughout the century was slow and patchy, but there *was* improvement, and as the demand for better transport grew so did men begin to realise the age-old dream of finding a mechanical substitute for animal power.

The first attempts to make 'horseless carriages' were based on the notion of using human power to work some kind of crank or treadmill which would then turn the wheels by toothed gearing, and it does not take an engineer's eye to see in all the elaborate contrivances drawn by inventors in this field that the power to weight ratio would have been hopelessly inadequate. Page 10 gives a good example of this kind of fantasy, and it is at once apparent that the unfortunate gentlemen on the treadmills on either side would have been grossly overworked; furthermore there is no means of steering. Leonardo da Vinci drew plans for an armoured fighting vehicle, shaped rather like a tortoise, with all four wheels driven by bevel gearing from a longitudinal crankshaft to be turned by four men; but even da Vinci, great genius though he was, ignored the steering problem and, as drawn, his bevel gears would have turned the two axles in opposite directions.

Sail driven cars were also proposed; some were actually built and used

NÜREMBURG-CARRIAGE

This Nüremburg processional state carriage must have meant hard work for the men who propelled it by means of tread-wheels.

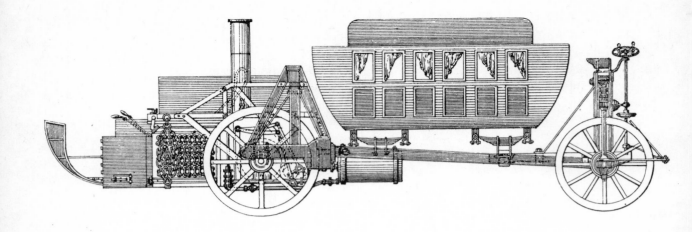

with a fair measure of success in flat country. A primitive form of the modern 'Ackermann' steering linkage is shown in connection with a wind-propelled carriage described in 1714, in the third volume of *Machines Approuvées par l'Academie des Sciences*, but it was in the numerous attempts, or proposals, to use clockwork that one finds the next real move towards the self-propelled carriage.

All such attempts were bound to fail; the clockwork motor only provides a way, and a very inefficient one, of storing up and re-using the muscular effort employed to wind up a spiral of flat elastic steel. Many would-be inventors fell into the error of supposing that a giant clock-spring and train of gear wheels could, in some mysterious way, increase the original effort, but despite this optimism the dictum that 'you can't get 'owt for nowt' prevails and, indeed, there is inevitably a loss rather than a gain of power in any mechanical contrivance. Therefore, despite many ambitious drawings and a few gallant practical attempts, the clockwork carriage remained an *ignis fatuus*. Towards the end of the last war, when petrol was strictly rationed and a few people had converted ordinary cars to burn producer gas, or into battery-electric machines, a reader wrote to one of the motoring journals suggesting the use of clockwork once again. His aspiration was crushed by the reply of the

GRIFFITH'S STEAM CARRIAGE, 1821

Steam carriage designed by Julius Griffiths in 1821 and built by Joseph Bramah, the celebrated inventor of the hydraulic press, the Bramah lock and many other things.

technical editor who took the matter with mock-seriousness, calculated all the details, and concluded that a car to carry four people at 10 miles an hour for twenty miles would require mainsprings totalling *five tons* in weight and that the effort of winding them, by human power through suitable reduction gearing, would take at least eight hours.

It was not, therefore, until the steam-engine became a practical proposition that the self-propelled carriage became a possibility rather than a pipe-dream. As a commercial proposition the steam engine dates from 1712 when Newcomen built his first atmospheric steam pumping machine, but many years before this scientists (including Sir Isaac Newton) had postulated the steam carriage. It is believed that Father Verbiest, one of the Jesuit priests at the Chinese Emperor's court, made a model steam carriage towards the end of the seventeenth century: this was probably little more than a toy though it appears to have depended upon the ultra-modern principle of jet-propulsion.

The Newcomen type of engine was worked by atmospheric pressure, and the steam was only employed to create a partial vacuum in the cylinder by condensation. The difficulties in the way of making precisely dimensioned cylinders, pistons and valves were equalled by the difficulties of making boilers, pipes and joints capable of standing more than a few pounds above atmospheric pressure; these constructional hurdles stood in the way of using high pressure steam expansively although the theoretical advantages of doing so were well understood, particularly after James Watt had investigated the atmospheric engine and made his notable improvements to it. Consequently Newcomen, or Watt-type, engines were too bulky, too heavy and too slow-moving to use for vehicle propulsion and Nicholas Joseph Cugnot, a Swiss engineer working for the French Government, deserves great credit for the experimental steam trucks he built between 1765 and 1770. They are, as far as we know, the first full-scale vehicles to be moved by mechanical power.

Cugnot's trucks were intended for carrying cannon, and he was subsidized by the French Government. With great ingenuity and daring he abandoned the atmospheric principle and made use of steam under pressure. His first experimental vehicle is said to have carried four passengers on its trial trip and to have moved quite steadily at about 3 m.p.h., but unfortunately he was dogged by the trouble which hampered

MURDOCK, 1781
William Murdock's model steam vehicle of 1781

so many early experimenters — the boiler was inadequate, and after about fifteen minutes work the truck ran out of breath and had to pause to build up a fresh head of steam.

Cugnot's second machine is still preserved in Paris (Page 17) and although the boiler now on it is not original and is, indeed, an unfinished and unusable affair, one can see how near this inventor came to finding a practical solution. To avoid geometric problems Cugnot used the tricycle layout, and used the front wheel for both driving and steering. This means that the whole weight of boiler and machinery has to pivot with the front wheel, but this arrangement, though needing great strength on the part of the steersman, is not quite so crude as it appears as Cugnot calculated that the load to be carried on the rear part of the truck, behind the steering pivot, would counterbalance the weight acting in front of the steering pivot. It is not clear at what pressure Cugnot intended to work his engine but it is known that he had great difficulty in getting the cylinders cast and bored with sufficient accuracy. Contemporary accounts refer to the '*pompes*' being faulty and this has been taken to mean that Cugnot had trouble with some kind of boiler feed-water pump. But the original writer, unversed in technical terms, was referring to the working cylinders, for the dimensions he quotes agree with those of the engine parts still to be found on the machine. The cylinders were 13" in bore, the pistons took a 12" stroke and turned the front wheel by a ratchet and pawl mechanism.

Writers have used their imaginations and drawn lurid word-pictures of the citizens of Paris flying in terror as Cugnot's monster snorted its way through the streets of Paris, finally getting out of control and knocking down a wall whereupon the hapless inventor was flung into jail and his machine confiscated. These picturesque stories are untrue: the trials were mostly conducted on private ground, and although a low brick wall *was* damaged (for which Cugnot was called to account, rather as one might be fined for a parking offence), the experiments were abandoned not because the inventor had been jailed but because a change of government policy cut off the supply of money needed for further development.

After Cugnot's excellent start nothing more was done in France for a long while, and the next developments took place in Britain which

JAMES, 1832

W.H. James's second steam carriage design of 1832. Not actually built. The specification included ingenious pedal-controlled 3-speed gear and gas lighting.

JAMES'S 4-CYL. MACHINERY, 1829

The 4-cylinder machinery of W. H. James's steam coach of 1829. There were, in effect, two separate 2-cylinder engines each driving one back wheel to allow for differential action when cornering. (Page 15, top)

HOLT, 1869

Holt's steam road carriage of 1869. A typical example of the second phase of steam carriage building in Britain; the Holt carriage ran well and was capable of about 20 m.p.h. but could not be developed because of the legal restrictions. (Page 15)

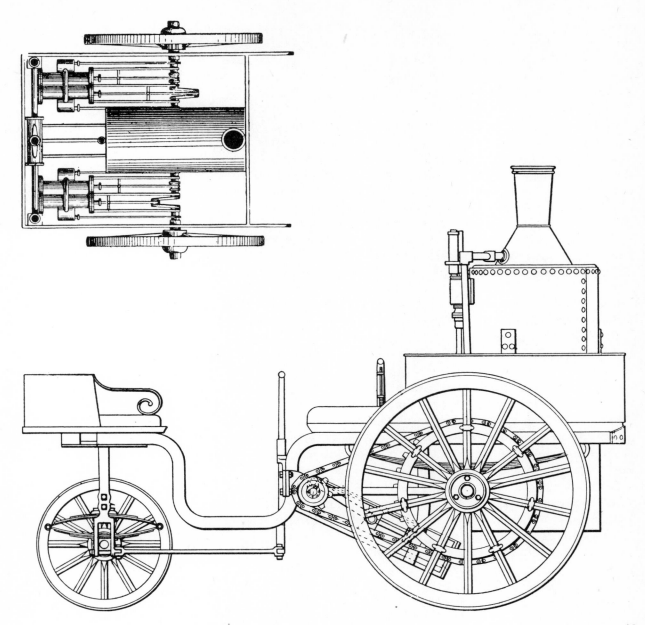

was, indeed, the home of the steam engine. England's lead may be measured by the fact that there were at least 5,000 steam engines at work in the mills and factories of Great Britain by 1820, in addition to the hundreds of pumping engines which allowed the mines to be driven ever deeper, whilst in France there were no more than 200 engines at work and fewer than 100 in Prussia.

James Watt himself took out a patent to cover steam road propulsion, laid down certain fundamental principles and made some sketches, but nothing came of these, and in the 1780's he frowned upon William Murdoch, his assistant, for trying to put these ideas into effect and Murdoch's experiments with an ingenious working model were sternly checked as a waste of time. It fell to Richard Trevithick, the great Cornish engineer, whose high pressure engines carried the steam engine forward from the point where Watt left off, to make the next real advance with two full-scale steam carriages which performed well.

Trevithick's first attempt, made in 1801, was little more than a boiler and engine on wheels, but his second vehicle had more of the carriage and less of the machine shop about it. We do not know exactly what it looked like for the well known drawing (Page 16) obviously owes more to the artist's imagination than to his eye for engineering detail. One cannot conceive, for example, how the passengers ever got into the coach body, nor are the steering arrangements very clear, but at least one can see that the engine was based on Trevithick's established high-pressure (approximately 60 lbs. per sq.in.) design, with the horizontal cylinder recessed into the boiler and with the cross head guides for the piston rod most ingeniously used to form the 'perch' or main chassis member of the carriage itself. An arrangement of spur gears provided a slow-speed for hills and a higher gear for use on the level.

In 1803 Trevithick had this engine dismantled and taken to London where it was re-assembled, fitted with body-work and made several demonstration trips: but though he showed that it was capable of running quite reliably, with a full load, at speeds up to 12 m.p.h. on the level, he could not find anyone to back him financially and had to turn his attention to other affairs.

This was the lot of other experimenters both in England and on the Continent: the ideas were there but the money was not. In America,

TREVITHICK, 1803
Richard Trevithick's 'London' steam carriage of 1803. This carriage ran very well but it was ahead of its time and the inventor could get no financial support to develop it.

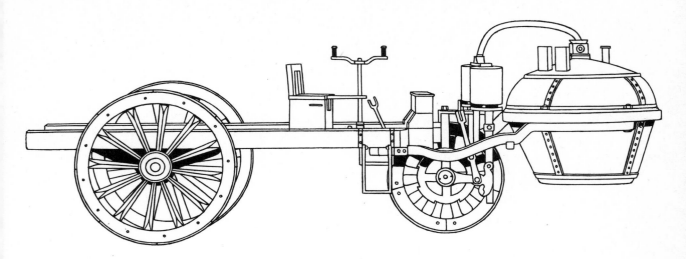

though there were very few steam engines in use before 1800, Oliver Evans was granted a licence to run steam waggons on the public highway as early as 1787, but his experiments did not bear much fruit. He is credited, incidentally, with inventing the first 'amphibian' which may be seen on Page 18; but this invention was purely fortuitous and what happened was that Evans was commissioned to build a self-propelling barge or pontoon for use in dock cleaning and repair work, and having built it he was faced with the problem of transporting it from the building shed to the water. His solution was to mount it upon a stout wheeled underframe and then to use the barge's own engine to propel the whole affair by means of pulleys and belts rigged up for the purpose.

Between 1820 and 1835 the steam road vehicle forged ahead and England was again the scene. Industrial expansion had been so rapid in England since about 1780 that the pressure on the inadequate transport system had become intolerable. Roads had improved and the stage coach system was very efficient; the canals, too, played their part, but horse-drawn land transport was inordinately expensive. Cartage by road in 1820 cost at least 2/- per ton-mile, and stage coach fares worked out at about 6 d. per mile. If these figures are translated into present day values it will be seen how industry was throttled and that only the well-to-do could afford to travel further than their legs could carry them.

CUGNOT, 1769-70
Joseph Cugnot's steam truck, probably finished in 1769/70 and still preserved in Paris.

From about 1820 onwards therefore, a number of engineers designed steam driven coaches which came within hailing distance of commercial success. They did not solve all the technical problems, though a little more time and experience would have sufficed, but when one considers that precision engineering on a large scale was in its infancy they were very successful.

Sir Goldsworthy Gurney, Sir Charles Dance, Walter Hancock, James Scott Russell, Burstall and Hill, William James were prominent among the many who made satisfactory mechanical carriages at this time. Some of them were used commercially, running scheduled services with fare-paying passengers. The best known were those run between Paddington and the Bank of England by Hancock, a shuttle service between Cheltenham and Gloucester operated by Sir Charles Dance using machines of Gurney's design, and the Glasgow to Paisley service operated by Scott Russell.

There were a few breakdowns, and moreover, all these steam coaches used a great deal of water, so that about ten miles was their limit before stopping to take on supplies; however, much had been learnt, particularly about making relatively light and compact quick-steaming high-pressure boilers. Much ingenuity was shown; in his second design of 1832, for instance, W. H. James proposed an ingenious 3-speed mechanism worked by chains and dog-clutches; Walter Hancock patented the 'artillery' wheel which flourished many years later, Hill patented (but did not use) the differential gear which was patented (and used) again in France a few months later and re-invented once more by Starley in 1872. In one way and another there was no reason why England should not have had a commercially viable system of steam road coaches by the 1840's. Inevitably, smaller carriages for private use—motor cars in effect—would soon have followed.

Two factors worked against them; the new-fangled railways, and opposition from the vast industry which had grown up round the horse. Not only did stage coach proprietors oppose them, but the thousands of drivers and grooms also were against them as well as farmers, hay and fodder merchants and land owners. These interests were particularly well represented on the Turnpike Trusts which administered the highways and their method was simple and deadly: they increased the tolls on

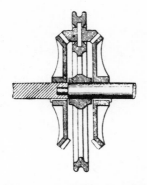

PECQUEUR'S DIFFERENTIAL GEAR, 1828

The differential gear used by Pecqueur in 1828; differential mechanism was used in elaborate clockwork in the sixteenth century and formed the basis of the 'South Pointing Chariot' invented in China before the Christian era.

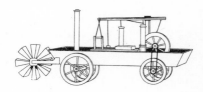

EVANS, 1805

Oliver Evans' dock-cleaning barge mounted on wheels to make, temporarily, a self propelled vehicle. 1805.

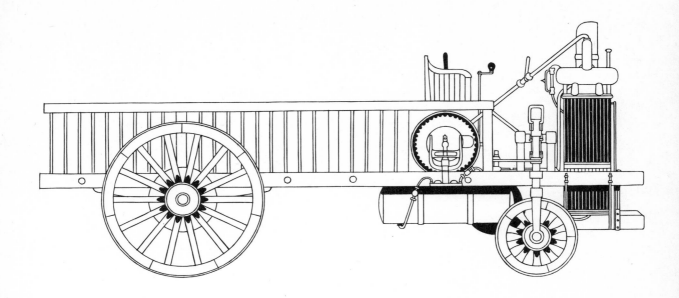

mechanical vehicles so much that it became uneconomic to use them. The new railways posed less difficult technical problems and promised a quicker return on capital. Consequently financial interests and the best engineering talents were drawn into the railways which grew and prospered between 1830 and 1860, whilst the road-steamer branch of transport withered away.

There was a brief revival in the late 1850's, and this time Parliament took a hand, on behalf of the railway companies which now had a near-monopoly, by passing a 'Locomotives on Highways Act' limiting the speed of mechanical vehicles to 2 m.p.h. in towns and 4 m.p.h. in open country. Further, every 'Road Locomotive' was to have three persons in attendance, one of whom must walk 60 yards ahead of the machine carrying a red flag by day and a red lantern by night.

This was the notorious 'Red Flag Act' which effectively put the brake on progress in Great Britain for forty years.

PECQUEUER, 1828

Onesiphore Pecqueur's steam truck of 1828 – a very advanced design with an efficient fire-tube boiler and differential gear.

It was also fitted with a form of Ackermann steering linkage and independent front wheel suspension on the 'sliding pillar' principle.

Chapter 2

THE START OF THE MOTOR INDUSTRY

The English steam coaches of the 1830's, and the experimental steam carriages which were built between 1840 and 1880 in England, France, Germany, Italy and America, were certainly automobiles but the modern motor car, as we know it, may be said to be a love-child born of the improbable union of a gas-engine with a tricycle.

The evolution of the bicycle from the heavy wooden framed and wooden-wheeled 'velocipede' of the 1860's, into the tubular iron framed, wire-wheeled 'ordinary' or 'penny-farthing' of the 'eighties and finally into the equal-wheeled, pneumatic tyred 'safety' of the 'nineties, gave to ordinary men of modest means the freedom to travel at will, untrammeled by set routes and time-tables, which had hitherto been reserved for the rich. The high bicycle, or 'ordinary', was quite unsuitable for women, but even before the safety bicycle appeared various forms of two-seat-tricycle or quadricycle had given women a taste for this freedom, at the cost of considerable muscular exertion, and many a cyclist must have dreamed of the day when some docile little machine, purring away beneath his saddle, would ease his aching muscles and allow him to conquer even more distant horizons. Although the first motor cars, and motorists, were generally unpopular the bicycle undoubtedly prepared the public mind, to some extent, to accept the horseless carriage.

MARKUS, 1875

Siegfried Markus' experimental petrol-engined car of 1875. It was restored to running order in 1949 and found capable of 8 m.p.h. on a level road.

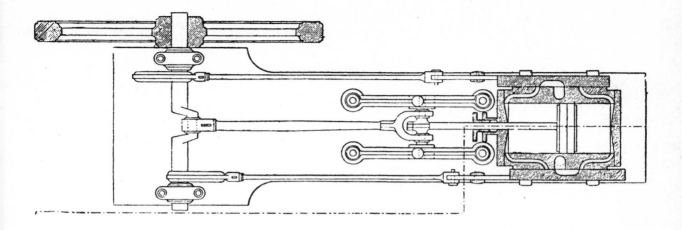

The idea of the internal-combustion engine is almost as old as that of the steam engine, but it was 1860 before the first commercially satisfactory gas engine was patented and put on the market by Etienne Lenoir. After that, progress was quite quick because, although the Lenoir type of engine was grossly inefficient, small businesses and workshops had need of some reasonably simple and handy source of power which could be started up at short notice and which needed no boiler or furnace man. The demand for Lenoir's engines (which were made under licence in other countries than France), stimulated other engineers and better types of gas engine were evolved; the most notable, from the motor car standpoint, being the 4-stroke engine designed by Gottlieb Daimler in 1876 on behalf of his employers, Messrs Otto and Langen of Deutz, and sold as the Otto Silent Gas Engine. It may be observed that the engine was silent only by comparison with the ear-shattering and foundation-shaking free piston atmospheric gas engine which Otto and Langen had sold before the 4-stroke motor made its bow.

In his patent specification Lenoir himself mentioned vehicle propulsion as one of the tasks for which his engine would be suitable, and he designed a surface vapouriser, or carburettor, to allow it to work on liquid fuel. In 1862 he actually constructed a very crude 'motor car' to

LENOIR'S GAS ENGINE, 1860
Plan view of Lenoir's gas engine, 1860.

21

show what his engine could do; but as it is recorded that he took six hours to cover the six miles between Paris and the suburb of Joinville one understands why he did not pursue the project further.

Nor, indeed, was Lenoir the first man to drive a vehicle by means of an internal combustion engine. Captain Brown of Brompton in London had demonstrated a carriage driven by his patent 'gas-vacuum' engine as early as 1824. Fifty years later Siegfried Markus of Vienna built a machine, the basis of which was little more than a converted hand cart, propelled by a 4-stroke petrol engine, which had several advanced features including a most ingenious carburettor and low tension magneto ignition. There were other experiments, but none of these ingenious innovators can claim the title of 'inventor' of the motor car as none of them went beyond isolated experiments which were quickly forgotten. If 'inventor' is taken to mean the man or woman who first pursues an idea to the stage of commercial production and public acceptance, however limited, Carl Benz of Mannheim has the best claim, although simultaneously and independently Gottlieb Daimler, with the help of his assistant Wilhelm Maybach, designed and patented the type of relatively high speed four stroke motor which is the direct ancestor of the modern automobile engine.

Benz was in business, in a small way, as a gas engine manufacturer and had patented a pump-scavenged two-stroke engine with electric ignition which sold quite well locally. Despite opposition from his partner he was determined to make a self propelled vehicle, and spent much of his time with experiments in 1884. Finding his 2-stroke engine rather too cumbersome for the job he designed a 4-stroke machine for the purpose (a legal ruling shortly before had found that the Otto and Langen patent for the 4-stroke principle had been anticipated by Beau de Rochas some ten years earlier; consequently Benz was not obliged to pay a royalty) and successfully united it with a tubular framed three wheeled chassis in 1885.

Benz's 4-stroke engine for his first car had one cylinder of 91.4mm bore by 150mm stroke; working with a compression ratio of 2.68 to 1 it developed 0.8 h.p. at 400 r.p.m. The inlet was controlled by a mechanical slide valve, similar to that used on steam engines, and the exhaust port was controlled by the normal kind of mushroom shaped poppet

valve still used to-day. The engine was water cooled though the car itself had no radiator, and the cooling water in the tank was just allowed to boil away. The electric ignition was looked after by primary battery and Ruhmkorpf trembler coil, and in typical stationary engine fashion the crank, connecting-rod and valve motion were all exposed and their lubrication was looked after by oil-and grease-cups. A simple surface carburettor, which also served as fuel tank, provided the inflammable mixture.

The engine was installed in the chassis horizontally, at the back, in such a way that the crankshaft was vertical and the large flywheel horizontally placed across the extreme width of the vehicle frame. It is usually said that Benz did this to obviate the effect of gyroscopic action upon the steering, but a more probable explanation is that he wanted to use the largest possible flywheel — one of those fitted to his stationary

LOCOMOBILE STEAM CAR, 1899

Locomobile steam car, designed by the twin Stanley brothers who sold the design to Locomobile. This type of very light petrol-burning steam runabout was popular at the turn of the century but was soon found to be too frail and troublesome for serious work.

engines—and found this the easiest way to accommodate it. At the upper end of the crank a pair of two-to-one ratio bevel gears gave motion to the cam and crank-pin which operated the valves and also to a large pulley from which an ordinary flat leather belt conveyed the power to a countershaft beneath the footboard: final drive was by side chains to the back wheels which revolved upon a 'dead' axle attached to the chassis by full-elliptic springs.

The countershaft had a differential gear of the modern type, but on this first car Benz used no change-speed mechanism. By means of a fixed and a free pulley on the countershaft, and the sort of striker fork then commonly found in the driving gear of factory machines, the belt could be guided from one pulley to the other so as to provide a clutch action for starting from rest, or a neutral position. The little machine ran, and ran quite well, and night after night Benz took it out and experimented with this, or adjusted that, until he was able to complete a circuit of the streets near his house without breakdown.

The gearing was such that the car could run at about 9 m.p.h. on the level, but this meant that with only $\frac{3}{4}$ h.p. available and no change speed gear, starting from rest quite often stalled the engine and the most gentle gradient would have been beyond the machine's power. The results were, however, so encouraging that Carl Benz set to and during the next two years made two or three more cars on the same general plan but with many improvements. The most notable changes were more powerful engines, a 2-speed chain-and-sprocket gear working on the countershaft, better brakes (those on the first car had been feeble to a degree) bigger storage tanks for cooling-water and fuel, wooden wheels in place of the wire spoked ones and more comfortable bodywork. These improved cars had a maximum speed of about 14 miles an hour and the low gear allowed them to start from rest with reasonable certainty, and (with a bit of luck) to climb gradients of 1 in 10.

So far, Benz had had no encouragement except from his wife and he had no idea of advertisement; his partner was no help, and was, indeed, furious, at the waste of time and money and threatened to withdraw from the business unless Benz would concentrate on the stationary engines which provided their bread and butter. In 1887 Benz exhibited his third pattern of car at the Paris Exposition where nobody showed the

DAIMLER ENGINE, 1885
Daimler's first 'high speed' (750 r.p.m.) engine of 1885.

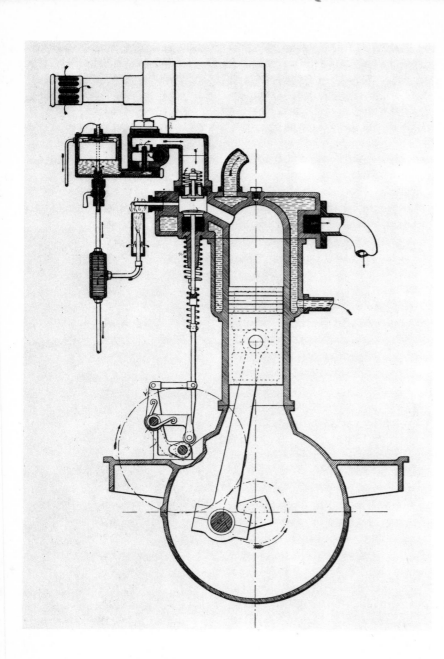

DAIMLER ENGINE, 1897

Cross section of a Daimler engine, c. 1897 showing the arrangement of the valves and the hot-tube ignition.

slightest interest in it, largely because no attempt was made to describe what it could do or to arrange demonstrations.

A few weeks later, however, a Parisian customer, who had already bought a Benz stationary engine to use in his workshop, heard about the motor car (he had, presumably, missed the Exposition) and went to Mannheim where he was given a trial trip on the car and promptly bought it. Not only did Benz sell the car but he appointed the buyer as the first motor agent in the world. Not only did Emile Roger, the buyer in question, become sole concessionaire for Benz cars in France, he was granted a licence to assemble cars in his own workshop in the Rue des Dames. In a small way the motor industry had started. Hitherto the only 'motorists' had been the experimenters themselves, but now any member of the public so foolish, so rash and so lost to all sense of the fitness of things as to wish for a horseless carriage could go to Roger in Paris or to Benz in Mannheim and order one.

Before considering the work of Daimler and others it will be convenient to take the Benz story up to 1901. Between 1888 and 1890 a few of the three wheeled cars were sold both by Benz and Roger, but Benz's successive partners remained hostile to the venture and withdrew from the little firm. Very fortunately Fritz von Fischer and Julius Ganss, who took their places, encouraged the motor car business and put more money into the concern.

With most of the weight concentrated over the back wheels the original three wheeled cars had been more than a little uncertain in their steering, and if they had been capable of more than about 14 m.p.h. there is little doubt they would have displayed a tendency to overturn on corners. In 1891, therefore, Benz re-designed the chassis to make a four wheeled car with Ackermann steering, controlled by a very neat arrangement of toothed pinion and racks operating a divided track-rod. At about the same time the engine was re-designed also; the vertical crankshaft was abolished and a smaller flywheel, rotating in the normal plane, took the place of the big horizontal flywheel. Two pulleys, of different diameters, were mounted on an extension of the crankshaft, beside the flywheel, and two sets of fast-and-loose pulleys on the countershaft and two sepa-ate belts, one for each pulley set, provided the low and high speeds. These modified engines could run up to the dizzy pace of some 700 r.p.m.

DAIMLER, 4-CYL. 1896
Daimler's first type of 4-cylinder engine, first used in 1896 but uncommon before 1898.

For the next ten years, although a variety of different models were offered, no major design changes were made and the differences between the models was chiefly a matter of size; even the 9h.p 2-cylinder car which appeared in 1898 (and was capable of 25 m.p.h.) was no more than an enlarged version of the original 4-wheeled design; and in the smaller class a 'Velo' of 1892, a 'Comfortable' of 1896 and an 'Ideal' of 1899 differ only in minor details. The horse-power ratings quoted for them are, incidentally, somewhat misleading. For example, the 'Velos' were advertised as $1\frac{1}{2}$ h.p. but their engine dimensions, of 110 x 110 mm, were the same as those of the later 'Ideals' which were called $3\frac{1}{2}$ h.p., and there is not enough difference in their respective performances to suggest that the one was more than twice as powerful as the other.

By 1901, indeed for some years before the end of the century, Panhard et Levassor and many others had outstripped Benz technically and some writers have poked fun at the little Benz carriages and at their reactionary creator for continuing so late with such a primitive, old-fashioned, design. Although it was incapable of much development beyond the initial stage the original Benz design had two great virtues — it worked extremely well, within its limitations, and it was so simple that the would-be motorist of the time who was, generally speaking, wholly ignorant of mechanical things, could easily see how it worked. For these reasons the Benz cars sold well and were widely copied.

A legitimate complaint was that they were not very good on hills; if the roads were soft in rainy weather it was by no means certain that a Benz could climb a 1 in 10 hill without a push from the passenger, and to overcome this difficulty many of the models, after 1898, were fitted with an emergency low-gear. This took the form of an epicyclic or ' crypto' gear built inside the 'loose' pulley of the high-speed gear and brought into action by a contracting brake or clutch. With the 'crypto' in action a Benz car could climb anything, though the occupants might die of old age before reaching the summit.

Although no doubt he clung on to his original design a little too long, it must be remembered that Carl Benz was not interested in the 'carriage trade'. He saw the automobile not as a rich man's toy, or as a means to sporting glory, but as a cheap and efficient substitute for the pony and trap. In terms of pony and trap transportation and cost he succeeded

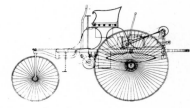

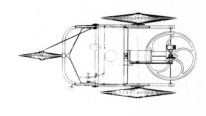

BENZ, 1885.
Elevation and plan views of Benz's experimental tricar of 1885. The horizontal flywheel can be seen, but in the plan drawing the steering pillar is shown on the right hand side of the car though, in fact, it was in the centre.

brilliantly, and although the little **Benz** cars of the 1890's may amuse one to-day by the mixture of ingenuity and perversity displayed in their design and construction, they were astonishingly reliable, all things considered, and even now one could set off on a thousand mile journey quite confident that one's patience would give way long before the machinery.

Many myths have been added to the history of the motor car, and one of them is that Carl Benz was one of Gottlieb Daimler's workmen and 'stole his secrets'. This is complete nonsense. The two pioneers never met; Daimler was the older man and died in 1900 at the age of 66, whilst Benz survived into his eighty fifth year and died in 1929. The only remote connection between them is that they both worked, at different times, for the Karlsruhe Maschinenbau.

In 1882 Daimler quarrelled with Otto and Langen, left the firm, moved to Cannstatt and set up an experimental workshop in his garden there. He was not always the easiest man to deal with, but there is little doubt he had good reason to feel disgruntled. Fortunately he was able to negotiate a reasonable settlement with Otto and Langen over the shares which had been awarded him in recognition of his contribution to the success of their business, so he was not too hard pressed for money. Equally fortunately he was able to persuade his right hand man, Wilhelm Maybach, to accompany him in his new venture.

The cause of the rift was that Dr. Otto opposed Daimler's plan to develop a much smaller, lighter and faster type of engine. The firm's big 4-stroke stationary engines were selling well and Otto could not agree that there would be scope for a much more compact machine, one specifically designed to run on liquid fuel so as to be independent of a gas supply. The stationary engines were pretty cumbersome in relation to the power they developed, and they ran at about 120 r.p.m. Daimler visualised something compact enough to use in pleasure boats, fire engines, light rail-cars or — who knows? — bicycles or carriages.

The first engine designed after Daimler and Maybach set up on their own was patented in 1883; the most notable feature was the 'hot-tube' ignition system (See Chapter 4) which was able to work much faster than the gas-jet and slide-valve system used on the stationary engines, whilst being simpler and more reliable than electric ignition by coil and

CEDERHOLM, 1894

This is the second of two experimental steam cars built in Sweden by the brothers Jöns and Anders Cederholm. The first car did not steer well as it lacked a differential gear and it was wrecked by colliding with a brick wall. The second car was much better, and had a 2-cylinder engine, differential gear and better steering arrangements. It ran fairly well but suffered from too small a condenser which set up back pressure and necessitated frequent halts to cool off.

battery which Benz favoured. Apart from this, the 1883 engine was no more that a scaled down horizontal gas engine with a surface carburettor to make it independent of a gas supply.

This was followed in 1885 by a vertical 'high speed' engine with, for the first time, a crank case and oil bath enclosing the crank pin and fly-wheels. This, too, was a completely self contained machine, with hot-tube ignition operated by the same fuel as the engine burnt and a sur-face carburettor mounted beside the cylinder. It was the direct ancestor of the modern motor car engine. The first engines of this type developed ½ h.p., were less than 30 inches high, weighed about 110 lbs and could run at some 600 r.p.m. This may seem pretty feeble by to-day's stan-dards but it was a notable advance, for example, over the original Otto and Langen atmospheric gas engines which, for a similar output, stood nearly seven feet high and weighed over a ton.

At this period Daimler was not concerned with the motor car as such; his idea was to demonstrate that the Daimler engine could be used for a great variety of purposes, and then to leave it to others to work out the best ways of applying it. Boats, tram and rail-cars, electric lighting sets, bicycles and carriages certainly came within his field of vision, but his wooden framed motor bicycle of 1885 and his motorised horse-carriage of the following year are crude in the extreme and much less prac-tical than Benz's first attempts, as they were merely intended as mobile demonstrations of the wonderful Daimler engine. The bicycle motor was air-cooled by forced draught from a fan blown round a casing over the cylinder, and the similar motor installed in the carriage has also been described as air-cooled by nearly every writer of motor history. An air-cooled engine may have been used at first, but photographs of the car clearly show a very neat tubular radiator behind the back seat, and pipes connecting it to the cylinder jacket. Though this experi-mental carriage would have been quite impractical for serious travelling, it was able to show on more than one occasion that the 1½ h.p. engine could propel four people at about 10 m.p.h. on a level road.

In 1889 the engine business was beginning to do well, and Daimler and Maybach constructed two more experimental cars. The first was a fairly large belt driven vehicle which, like that of 1886, had a centre-pivoted front axle for steering; this system works well on a horse-drawn

THE HAMMEL, 1886

The Hammel, built in Denmark in 1886, powered by a 2-cylinder horizontal engine developing about 3 h.p., and used by the designer for many years to drive between work and home.

vehicle as the leverage of the shafts and the pull of the horse counteract the tendency of the axle to swing round if one wheel strikes a bump or stone, but it is a most unsuitable form of steering for any but the slowest of mechanical vehicles. The second of the 1889 experiments was of more significance; it was a tubular framed quadricycle, with Ackermann steering linkage and sliding-pinion change speed mechanism. Both of these cars were driven by the latest pattern Daimler engine which had two cylinders arranged in a narrow angle V formation, and which developed $3\frac{1}{2}$ h.p. at 700 r.p.m.

Whilst all this was going on in Cannstatt, things were also moving ahead in Paris where many inventors were toying with self-propelled carriages most of which were driven by steam. Léon Serpollet, who reinvented the 'flash' boiler about this time, and Count de Dion with his employees, Bouton and Trépardoux, were prominent figures in the steam carriage world whilst Roger kept the internal-combustion flag flying with his Roger-Benz carriages.

Daimler had sold the French patent and manufacturing rights in his engines, in 1886, to Edouard Sarazin, a Belgian solicitor. To comply with French law it was necessary that engines should be made throughout in France and not merely assembled from imported parts; consequently Sarazin agreed with his friend Emile Levassor that the newly founded engineering concern of Panhard and Levassor should have the right to manufacture French Daimler engines.

This agreement scarcely had time to take effect before Sarazin died (in December 1887), and his rights in the patents passed to his widow. During a visit she made to Cannstatt soon after her husband's death Mme. Sarazin so impressed Gottlieb Daimler with her ability that he agreed to transfer all his interests in France to her (in return, of course, for the usual royalties), and she in her turn confirmed the manufacturing agreement with Panhard et Levassor. The business-like widow consolidated the arrangement in 1890 by marrying Emile Levassor; the stage was set for the great French domination of the automobile world during the next ten years.

A FAMOUS LETTER

A facsimile of the letter Gottlieb Daimler wrote to the newlywidowed Mme. Sarazin confirming his agreement to let her carry on the Daimler business in France.

Cannstatt le 4 Janvier 1888

Chère Madame Sarazin;

L'année passée n'a pas bien finie pour nous. votre nouvelle,
que votre cher mari, notre bon Monsieur Sarazin n'est plus
m'a tout à fait étonné; je ne peux pas vous dire, combien
que je le déplore, il me faut toujours penser à lui et
regretter, que si n'ai pas faite plutôt ma visite promise
à Paris pour que nous nous eussions pu encore une
fois nous voir dans cette vie et nous serrer les mains
Maintenant tout est trop tard et je puis seulement
à vous dire encore. l'expression de mes sentiments et de
mon regret Je me fais des reproches, que peut-être je lui
ai fait des inquiétudes dans ses derniers jours par mes affaires
mais je n'avais pas une idée de sa maladie. seulement je
trouvais son écriture un peu changé. j'aimerais bien
vous voudriez dans votre prochain me dire quelquechose de sa
maladie et derniers jours.

Chance played its part in selecting Messrs Panhard et Levassor as the men responsible for making the Daimler type of engine outstandingly successful in the first place, and it was to a great extent fortuitous that the design of motor car Emile Levassor hit upon in 1891 should have decided the basic form of the conventional vehicle until comparatively recently.

It may be assumed that most of the men running the small engineering concerns in and around Paris kept their eyes upon the attempts being made by De Dion and others to make the automobile a commercial proposition. It is certain that Emile Levassor examined one of the Roger-Benz carriages, and it seems that he did not think much of it. He visited the little factory Daimler and Maybach had set up in Cannstatt, in 1890, and examined the bicycle and the three experimental cars there. He appears to have thought pretty poorly of them on the whole, though he approved of the sliding-gear change-speed mechanism on the quadricycle; yet on his own first essay in motor car design, made later in the year, he used belts and pulleys for the change-speed gear.

The first Panhard-Levassor motor car had the Daimler V-twin engine placed vertically and transversely in the centre of the frame, with back-to-back seating arranged over it. During the course of experiments this

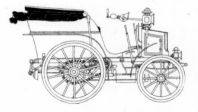

PANHARD-LEVASSOR, 1895

The 2-cylinder 4 h.p. Panhard-Levassor car in which Emile Levassor drove for $48^3/_4$ hours to be first home in the Paris-Bordeaux-Paris Race of 1895.

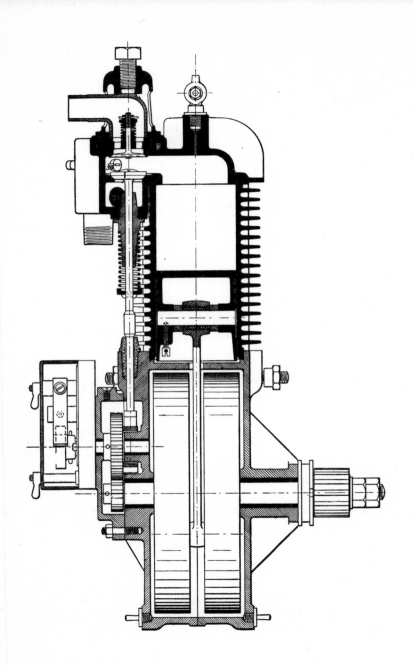

DE DION ENGINE, 1898

Cross-section of De Dion Bouton engine, 1898. By machining to close limits and by careful attention to weight reduction Georges Bouton was able to raise the normal working speed, and consequently the efficiency, of the De Dion Bouton engines far above the average of the time.

machine was altered so many times that it is pointless to describe it in detail, but after a relatively short while Levassor decided that belt transmission, admirably quiet and simple though it was, was not really the best solution. Early in 1891 he constructed an entirely new type of motor car.

No longer was the engine placed partly under the seats, or at the back of the frame, but vertically in the front of the chassis, covered by a kind of cupboard, immediately behind the front axle. Moreover the crankshaft was parallel with the longitudinal line of the vehicle instead of parallel with the axles as had been the case with all previous designs. This meant that bevel gears (or some other form of right-angled drive) were needed at some point in the transmission, but had the great advantage that when the time came to use bigger and more powerful engines it was relatively easy to accommodate them. The power was transmitted through a pedal-controlled friction clutch to a three speed sliding-pinion change-speed gear which was not enclosed, and which was, in consequence, lubricated by grease, road dust and optimism in equal proportions. From the second-motion shaft the drive went to a bevel geared cross shaft and finally by chain to a differential live axle. This last detail was subsequently altered; the differential mechanism was moved to the countershaft and the final drive taken by side chains (in the Benz manner) to the hind wheels revolving on a dead axle. This made for a lighter but sturdier axle and constitutes the only major change in the layout which soon came to be called the *système Panhard* (*système Levassor* might seem more just), from which the conventional twentieth century motor car evolved.

The controls consisted of a 'cow's tail' tiller for steering, a hand lever to work contracting brakes on the back wheel hubs and to disengage the clutch at the same time, a second lever to select neutral, forward or reverse (by transferring the drive from one bevel pinion on the countershaft to another), a third lever moving over a segment of a circle to select the three speeds, a pedal to work the clutch and a second pedal to operate a band brake on the countershaft. As with the hand brake, this was inter-connected with the clutch withdrawal linkage so that use of either brake automatically declutched the engine. This would seem pointless and dangerous to the modern motorist, but as the early

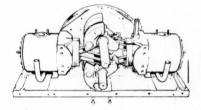

LANCHESTER ENGINE, 1900/5
Lanchester's 2-cylinder vibration-less engine, used 1900-05. There were two superimposed crankshafts, each with a flywheel, rotating in opposite directions. These were geared together and linked to the two 5¼ inch diameter pistons by six connecting rods. The engine was completely balanced by reverse rotation.

engines were not throttled, but tried always to run as near their maximum set speed as the load would permit the arrangement was really quite logical. Engine speed was controlled by a centrifugal governor which prevented the exhaust valves from opening if a certain speed (about 750 r.p.m.) was exceeded, and the only control the driver could exert was by means of a screw device on the dashboard which allowed him to override the governor and permit the engine to run faster than normal. Towards the end of the decade this control was pedal-operated and the name 'accelerator' was applied to it.

With an engine that tended always to work at its peak speed when the load permitted, changing gear with M. Levassor's system of sliding one toothed wheel into mesh with another, both revolving at different peripheral speeds, was a hazardous and noisy business. For many years, even when engines had become more flexible, phrases like 'the clashing and jarring of changing speeds', or 'prolonged side grubbing of teeth', constantly occur in motoring journals and manuals. Levassor is alleged to have said of his arrangement: '*c'est brutal mais ça marche*', and march it did to remarkably good effect.

Naturally enough many breakdowns and mishaps beset the first motorists, but many of their troubles were attributable to bad roads, tyre failures and their own total ignorance of machinery; but allowing for these factors the early Panhard-Levassor cars were astonishingly reliable. One of the very first to be sold, in December 1891, was still in daily use in 1912, having come into the hands of an impoverished country clergyman who reckoned that he had driven it 36,000 miles without serious trouble during his eighteen years of ownership.

Benz is derided for sticking so long to his original design but Levassor is praised as a more 'advanced' motor engineer because his arrangement (largely by chance) provided the essential basis for future development. This is not to belittle his achievement, yet in effect Levassor made as few fundamental changes as Benz in the decade 1891-1901.

The change in final drive arrangements has already been mentioned and after 1894 the change-speed and countershaft gears were decently enclosed; but the method of reversing, by shifting the countershaft bevels, remained in use until nearly the end of the century. This meant that Panhard-Levassor cars had as many speeds in reverse as they had for-

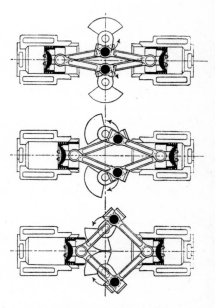

LANCHESTER-SYSTEM

Three phases in the compound motion of the pistons and cranks of Lanchester's vibrationless 2-cylinder engine.

wards. Most of the cars after the first three years were furnished with four speeds instead of three, but on all of them there was no 'direct drive' (an innovation attributed to Renault) and on all gears the drive was indirect. Other innovations were that after 1893 the new Maybach spray carburettor was used in place of the surface vapouriser; rather ineffective radiators (fitted, at first, at the back of the chassis) were used to supplement the cooling water tank after 1896 and the tiller steering was given up in favour of worm and wheel gear after 1897. By this time speeds had risen enough to show up the weakness of the original arrangement, and Levassor himself died in 1897 as a result of internal injuries sustained when he lost control of the steering and overturned during the Paris-Marseilles Race of the previous year.

The most significant change in the engine department was made in 1895, when Levassor first used the new pattern Daimler 'Phoenix' engine in which the two cylinders were arranged tandem fashion, one behind the other, instead of in a V-formation. With the first of the cars equipped with the new engine, which was of 80 mm bore and 120 mm stroke and developed 4 h.p. (French rating) at 750 r.p.m., Levassor performed his memorable feat of driving for $48^3/_4$ hours, with no relief driver, to be first home in the Paris-Bordeaux-Paris Race at an average speed of 15 m.p.h. over the formidable distance of 732 miles. Levassor's physical stamina was equalled by the unfaltering reliability of his engine — the longest halt for oiling and adjustment was of only 22 minutes duration — and lifted Panhard-Levassor's reputation to first place in the tiny motoring world of the time.

For, by 1895, there was a 'motor world' and Paris was its centre. Germany may be the birth-place of the motor car but France was its nursery. The French national temperament at that time seems to have been particularly well adapted to the new age and where, in Britain, Germany and America, official opposition combined with the conservatism of the 'carriage gentry' to hinder the new locomotion, the French authorities were very much less restrictive and the French public, in general, less hostile.

One of the factors which helped the infant motor car to develop was the growth of a well-informed and encouraging technical press. As early as 1887 M. Fossier, editor and owner of the *Vélocipede*, organised a

HORSELESS HANSOM
Hautier electric cab, 1899.

public demonstration of mechanical vehicles. It cannot be called a striking success as the only motor car to appear was the Count de Dion's little steam quadricycle which was driven up and down the short course with considerable *élan*; but M. Fossier's effort was, at least, in marked contrast to the scorn and hostility of the bicycling press in most other countries.

One of the great French sporting events, then as now, was the annual long-distance bicycle race, organised at that time by *Le Petit Journal*; in 1892 Peugeot followed the race in one of the first of his Daimler engined motor cars, and succeeded in covering the 1,500 miles of the Paris-Brest-Paris course at an average speed of 10 m.p.h. This was a remarkable effort which so impressed Pierre Giffard, editor of *Le Petit Journal* that he announced in his paper in December 1893 that the contest for 1894 would be, not a bicycle race, but a *Concours des Voitures sans Chevaux*. This took the form of an exhibition on July 18th, followed by some eliminating trials and culminating in a timed Reliability Run from Paris to Rouen (78 miles) on the 22nd of July.

The interest in horseless carriages had grown to such a degree, and the publicity given to the affair was so great, that every engineering crackpot in France, it seems, submitted an entry. Amongst the 102 vehicles entered were strange and terrible figments of disordered imagination to be propelled by 'Weight of Passengers', 'Constant Propulsion Motor', or a 'Combination of Gas and Pendulum'; Messrs Desoignes de Malapert et Barriere proposed the use of '*Liquides combinés*', which suggests they had been mixing their drinks, whilst Messrs Garnier et Delannoy pinned their faith to a 'Combination of Animate and Mechanical Motor' — whatever that might mean.

Needless to say, none of these improbable devices materialised; out of the twenty one vehicles which actually started on the run to Rouen thirteen were driven by internal combustion engines and the remainder by steam. All the petrol cars finished the course, though four of the large steamers (delivery vans or omnibuses rather than private cars) broke down.

The affair was not supposed to be a race, but the public fancy was caught by the ebullient Count de Dion who was first to arrive at Rouen, (having travelled at times at some 30 m.p.h.), despite spending longer at

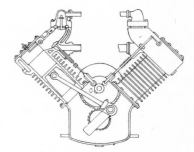

MORS, 1898
Mors cars of 1898 had a 4-cylinder engine of V-formation with air-cooled cylinder barrels and detachable water-cooled heads.

the luncheon stop than anyone else and then loosing more time by running off the road and having to be dug out of a potato patch. His vehicle was a De Dion, Bouton et Trépardoux 'Steam Horse'; that is, a light high-speed tractor drawing a landau from which the fore-carriage had been removed so that the two vehicles together comprised a six wheeled articulated unit.

After this auspicious start it was almost inevitable that the next step would be a proper speed contest. Giffard was eager to organise a race but M. Marinoni, proprietor of *Le Petit Journal*, was afraid of falling foul of the authorities if his paper were associated with racing on the public roads and anything went wrong; consequently an independent committee was set up at Count de Dion's instigation. This committee in due time resolved to constitute itself as a permanent body to encourage automobilism and to regulate all sporting events connected with it. In this way the *Automobile Club de France*, the first motor club in the world, was founded early in 1895. This was the body responsible for the Paris-Bordeaux-Paris Race in which Emile Levassor so distinguished himself. Thereafter the Road Races, Hill-Climbs, Reliability Runs and other contests organised by the A.C.F. became of the greatest consequence to the development of the motor car and helped to make France the leading nation in automobile matters until well past the turn of the century. Further details of the early motor races will be found in Chapter 5.

Space does not allow detailed descriptions of all the motor cars, steam, petrol or battery-electric, turned out by hopeful inventors and small engineering concerns in France during the 1890's. Some of these fell by the wayside through sheer bad luck, or lack of commercial aptitude, others fell because of sheer bad design or construction and a number survived to become twentieth century rivals to Panhard-Levassor — *La Marque Doyenne*.

Léon Serpollet, who was, after 1898, financed by a rich American called Gardner, became acknowledged king in the steam car field, whilst Jeantaud led the way down the short but attractive blind-alley of the battery-electric car. These two branches of the automotive tree did not prosper as their protagonists hoped; but when, for the first time, the magic speed of 60 m.p.h. was exceeded (in 1899) it was by an electric

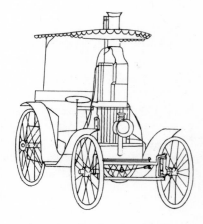

BOLLÉE'S LIGHT STEAM CARRIAGE, 1885

A light steam carriage built by Amédée Bollée, junior, in 1885.

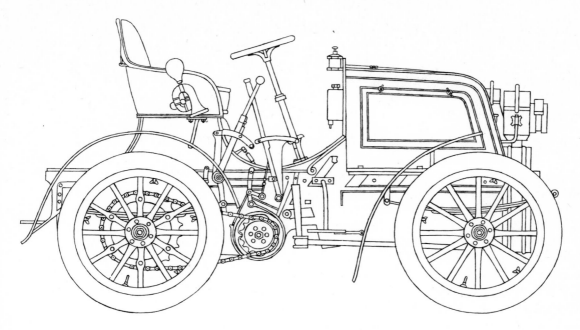

car. Steam car successes in hill climbs and speed record attempts, and some remarkable near-misses in full-scale long-distance racing, also helped to confirm the opposition of those who thought the petrol-engined vehicle, with its complicated transmission system, its noise, its vibration and its smell, would never find favour with the public. As year succeeded year, however, the petrol car gained ground despite its theoretical disadvantages.

A number of firms started making motor cars by the simple expedient of copying the Benz design, either more or less exactly, or with no more than a distant bow in the direction of Mannheim. This copying was not only done in France: Arnold, International, Marshall and Star were English practitioners on the Benz theme; Müller in New York and Lutzmann (amongst others) in Germany also followed suit, whilst in France the list was formidable. It included Hurtu, Georges Richard, Rochet-Schneider, Parisienne, Rossel, Fisson, Triouleyre and a few more. Of these, the first three broke away from their Benz origins and became well known in the twentieth century; Georges Richard, for instance,

'PHOENIX' DAIMLER, 1899
The 24 h.p. 4-cylinder 'Phoenix' Daimler racing car of 1899. This was the immediate predecessor of the first Mercedes model of 1900/01. Mechanical features include the 'gate' gear change, honeycomb radiator, steel girder chassis and low tension magneto ignition.

39

dominated both London and Paris with his 'Unic' taxi-cabs for many years.

Although the Daimler rather than the Benz type of engine soon proved superior, the Panhard-Levassor example was not, at first, widely followed. Rossel built one or two Daimler-engined cars and so did Lebrun but it fell to the Peugeot brothers to become Panhard-Levassor's principal customers for Daimler-type engines.

The young Peugeot — *Le fils de Peugeot frères de Valentigny* — came into the motor industry more or less by chance, as so many did. Armand Peugeot spent some time in England learning the trade and then persuaded his father and uncle to add bicycle building to the family firm's general ironmongery business in 1885. Four years later he collaborated with Serpollet in making a large three-wheeled tubular-framed carriage, powered by a Serpollet instantaneous steam generator, or 'flash boiler', and engine. In June 1890, accompanied by Serpollet and Ernest Archdeacon, Peugeot succeeded in driving this machine from Paris to Lyons.

As the 300 mile journey took five and a half days, during which practically everything which could break or give trouble did so, it is not surprising that Peugeot considered the steam plant too heavy, and thought it might be worth while experimenting with one of the new-fangled 'explosion' engines. Consequently the next Peugeot was lighter, had four wheels and was propelled by a Daimler engine bought from Messrs. Panhard et Levassor.

At first, a Benz type of belt-and-pulley transmission was used, but this was soon abandoned in favour of a friction clutch and sliding gears in the Panhard-Levassor manner; the great differences being, however, that Peugeot did not copy the Panhard-Levassor forward-mounted engine but favoured keeping the machinery at the back. Also, the Peugeot cars always looked, and generally were, rather lighter, with their tubular framing and wire wheels, than the rather clumsy looking Panhards with their timber chassis and carriage wheels. A peculiarity of the first Peugeot cars was that the cooling water was circulated through the tubular chassis which thus served as a radiator. This idea was, perhaps, copied from Daimler's quadricycle of 1889 which had a similar arrangement; after a while conventional gilled-tube radiators were fitted, but the chassis side members continued to be used as water pipes.

KNIGHT, 1896
J. H. Knight's experimental car. Built as a three-wheeler in 1894/5 and altered to 4-wheels in 1896. In this form it has independent front wheel suspension.

DAIMLER, 1886

Daimler's first experimental motor-car with
1-cylinder vertical water-cooled engine installed in converted horse-carriage. 2-speed.
primary transmission by belt and pulley,
final drive by pinions to gears on back
wheels. Hot-tube ignition. Claimed maximum speed 9 m.p.h. Germany.

BENZ, 1888

1-cylinder, 1½ h.p. horizontal engine, with
vertical crankshaft and horizontal flywheel. Primary drive by belt and pulley
to 2-speed chain gearing on countershaft
and final drive by chain. Electric ignition,
water cooling with no radiator - water
from storage tank gradually boiled away.

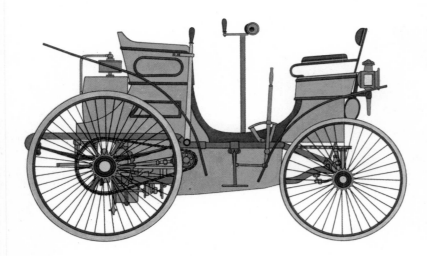

PEUGEOT, 1893

2½ h.p. Daimler-type. V-twin engine, rear
mounted. Cone clutch and 4-speed and
reverse sliding-pinion gearbox. Final drive
by chains. France.

DURYEA, 1894-1895

1-cylinder horizontal engine (original experimental Duryea car had 2-stroke unit). 2-speed belt-and-pulley primary transmission. This car won America's first authentic motor race - the "Times-Herald" contest - in November 1895. USA.

LANCHESTER, 1895

Lanchester's first car, originally with single cylinder, 5 h.p. engine, but shown here as rebuilt early in 1897 with horizontally opposed two cylinder, double crankshaft vibrationless engine of 8 h.p. Low-tension magneto ignition.

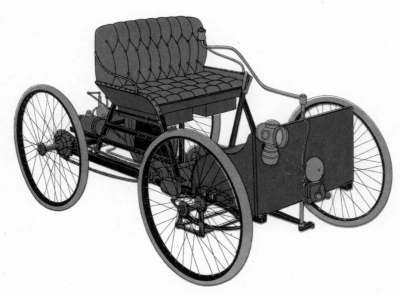

FORD, 1896

Ford's first experimental car. 2-cylinder horizontal engine. Two speed primary drive by belts and jockey pulleys. No brakes. No reverse gear. Top speed about 17 m.p.h. USA.

DAIMLER, 1896

2-cylinder vertical rear-mounted engine,
rated at 4. h.p., hot-tube ignition, primary
drive and 4-speed mechanism by belts and
jockey-pulleys. Final drive by spur gears,
steering by centre-pivot axle. Water cooling
with early form of honeycomb radiator
(possibly a later addition). Maximum speed
approx. 16 m.p.h. Germany.

RENAULT, 1898

2¼ h.p. De Dion Bouton engine. Apart
from the engine the whole car was designed by Louis Renault with his patented
"tumbler-action". 3-speed and reverse gearbox and jointed propeller shaft driving
bevel geared live axle. France.

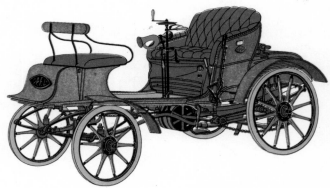

The Opel brothers took over Lutzmann and began, in 1901, building Darracq cars under license, but during 1900 continued producing a modernised version of Lutzmann (shown here) which was, in fact, based on the Benz design. 4 h.p. horizontal engine at rear, 2-speed belt primary drive, final drive by chains. Maximum speed approx. 14 m.p.h. Germany.

DE DION BOUTON, 1901

1-cylinder vertical rear-mounted engine (3½ h.p. at 1,500 r.p.m.). Driving by patented constant mesh. 2-speed gear (Each gear engaged gently by its own expanding clutch). Final drive by spur gear and De Dion system of universally-jointed half shafts, driving wheels carried on curved tubular "dead" axle. France.

DAIMLER, 1897

Alongside his rear engined belt-driven carriages Daimler built a variety of more modern vehicles including this 5 h.p. 2-cylinder car with front-mounted engine and sliding-gear change-speed mechanism similar to the Panhard-Levassor. Germany.

COLUMBIA, 1901

1-cylinder vertical engine, 5 h.p. 3-speed
and reverse sliding-pinion gearbox. Top
speed about 28 m.p.h. Shaft drive to live
axle. Automatic advance-and-retard ignition mechanism. Designed by Hiram
Maxim, junior. USA.

FIAT 16/24 H.P., 1903

4-cylinder engine, 24 h.p. Low-tension
magneto ignition. Chain driven. Top speed
about 50 m.p.h. Fabbrica Italiana Auto-
mobili Torino was started 1899, based
their later designs upon the Mercedes.
Italy.

MERCEDES 1902

The 40 h.p. (35 P.S.) 'Mercedes-Simplex'
was a refined and enlarged version of the
1901 prototype Mercedes model; it had a
5.3 litre 4-cylinder engine with mechanical
inlet valves and low tension magneto
ignition, driving through the Mercedes
patent scroll clutch to a 4-speed gearbox
with selective, or 'gate' control. There were
no fewer than five control pedals.

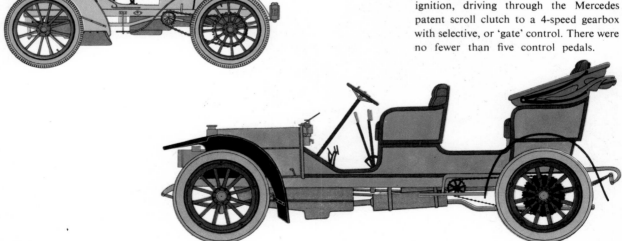

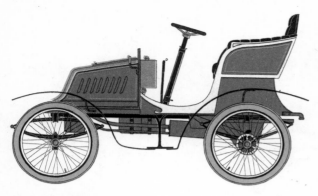

BIANCHI PHAETON, 1903

8 h.p. at 1,500 r.p.m. Weight about 772 lbs. One of the many makes of small car powered by the famous De Dion Bouton single-cylinder engine. Italy.

OPEL DARRACQ, 1902

1-cylinder engine. Swept vol. 78 cu.ins. 9 h.p. at 1,200 r.p.m. 3-speed gearbox and universally jointed propeller shaft and live axle. Built under licence. Germany.

FORD A, 1903

2-cylinder engine. Swept vol. 105 cu.ins. 8 h.p. at 1,000 r.p.m. The engine was under the seat with transverse crankshaft in the accepted style of the light American "gas-buggy" of the period USA.

CADILLAC, 1902/03

1-cylinder horizontal engine, 9.9 h.p. at
800 r.p.m. 2-speed and reverse epicyclic
gear and single chain to live axle. USA.

THE LITTLE SIDDELEY, 1904

1-cylinder horizontal engine, 6 h.p. cone clutch, primary drive by chain. 3-speed reverse gearbox. Final drive by chain. Except for radiator and bonnet this is identical with contemporary Wolseley and was built by Wolseley Co. Designed by Herbert Austin. Great Britain.

These rear-engined cars soon began to score successes, but the older members of the Peugeot family looked askance at the motor business and a separate concern was set up under Armand's direction. The Peugeot cars would have been awarded first prize in the Paris-Rouen Trial had it not been pointed out that their engines had been bought ready made from Panhard et Levassor who thus showed greater originality. The prize was, in consequence, equally divided between the two firms. In the following year, although Emile Levassor was the undoubted hero of the Paris-Bordeaux-Paris Race, Peugeot carried off first prize, though the winning Peugeot was some eleven hours behind Levassor, as the regulations reserved the premier award for a 4-seater vehicle and the triumphant Panhard-Levassor had but two seats.

After 1896 Peugeot gave up depending on their rivals for engines and designed their own horizontal unit which was better suited than the vertical Daimler engine to being carried at the back of the chassis. For their racing cars the engines were steadily enlarged until, by 1899, they had reached the impressive dimensions of a 2-cylinder engine of 140 mm bore by 190 mm stroke (5,850 cc) which probably developed about 22 h.p. As the only practicable method of getting more power then was by increasing the dimensions of the engine this represented the limit to which the rear engined Peugeot could be developed — it was a physical impossibility to cram more power into the space available, and in the new century Peugeot joined the majority in following Panhard-Levassor's example.

Count Albert de Dion, who succeeded his father as Marquis in 1901, was a very large man of great character whose influence on the development and acceptance of the motor car, technically, commercially and socially, was prodigious. He was an aristocrat, a gambler, a duellist and a gourmet who enjoyed all that his position in society made possible; yet at the same time he possessed sound commercial sense and a scientific turn of mind.

The possibility of making steam carriages light and handy enough for private use intrigued him, and in 1881 he hired Messrs. Bouton et Trépardoux, brothers-in-law and jobbing engineers in a small way of business, to work on his ideas. His choice of the brothers-in-law followed his purchase of a fascinating little toy steam engine, which had a glass cylin-

MORS, 1901

1901 7 h.p. 2-cylinder Mors — with Sewell's patent puncture-proof tyres.

der and which was so beautifully made that he persuaded the shopkeeper to tell him who had supplied it. He was directed to Bouton and Trépardoux's workshop and decided they were the right people to work for him, and as their model making and other work barely yielded a living Georges Bouton was ready enough to accept his offer of eight francs a day to work on his crackpot schemes. M. Trépardoux, a morose and pessimistic individual, was less enthusiastic but agreed to join the venture none the less.

During the next dozen years a number of steam carriages, tricycles, quadricycles, omnibuses and so forth were constructed; some were actually used commercially and the association between the Count and his engineers became a partnership.

Their later steam vehicles were extremely ingenious and included two notable inventions. These were the Bouton boiler, which was a light, compact and quick steaming water-tube affair, and a most ingenious arrangement of final drive and rear axle mechanism which was probably designed by Trépardoux. Under the name of the 'De Dion axle' this final drive system has been revived in recent years and used with great success on various cars and lorries.

Though the steamers which bore his name were mechanically satisfactory the Count was business-man enough to see that a coke- or coal-fired vehicle, which needed a *chauffeur*, or stoker, could not be acceptable as a light private carriage. Liquid fuel burners, with all the attendant automatic thermostatic devices to do the stoker's work, were then in the experimental stage, and de Dion saw that the internal combustion engine, despite its inflexibility and its tantrums, would suit his purpose better than steam. Between 1889 and 1892 he sketched designs for some remarkably advanced four- and twelve-cylinder rotary petrol engines. Bouton shared his views but Trépardoux, a steam-engine man to the core, uttered gloomy prophecies of doom through the curtain of a heavy walrus moustache. Because of his opposition, experimental work on petrol engines was done for de Dion by one Delalande at first; but during 1893/4 a petrol engine was developed by Georges Bouton in their own workshop.

This was too much for poor M. Trépardoux: 'To work upon the explosion engine is to work against ourselves' he declared. He left the other

PANHARD-LEVASSOR, 1892/3

An early production model Panhard-Levassor, 1892/3 type with the V-twin Daimler engine, made by Panhard-Levassor. This engine developed about 4 h.p. and gave the car a top speed of 18 m.p.h.

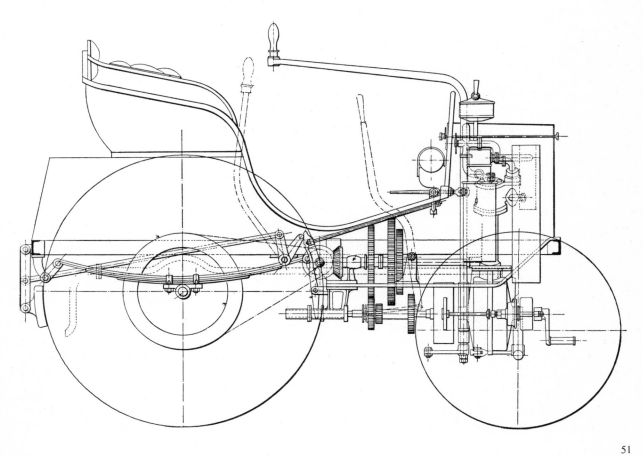

two partners to pursue their follies, and in so doing he also left the chance of sharing in the great prosperity which de Dion and Bouton were to enjoy a little later.

The first De Dion Bouton petrol engine was run on test towards the end of 1894: it was a tiny air-cooled single cylinder machine of 50 mm bore by 70 mm stroke (137 c.c.) and tricycles fitted with similar, but slightly larger, engines began to leave the factory in 1895.

The great importance of de Dion and Bouton's contribution to the development of the motor engine is that they carried Daimler's principal the next logical step forward. The Daimler type of engine, running at 700-800 r.p.m., was regarded as a high speed affair — which it was by comparison with the Benz type — but the first De Dion engines had a normal working speed of 1,500 r.p.m. and could run at double that pace (then thought fantastic) for brief periods without bursting. These high speeds, which helped to raise efficiency, were made possible by careful attention to the weight reduction and accuracy of the reciprocating parts, thereby keeping inertia stresses at a minimum, and by a new form of contact mechanism which Bouton devised to allow an electric ignition system to function at high speeds without misfiring.

The first tricycle engines developed about $^3/_4$ h.p. which represents about 4 h.p. per litre: by 1896 engines of 250 c.c. were being used and these were rated at $1^3/_4$ h.p. which equals some 7 h.p. per litre. The specific output therefore was about double that of the Daimler engine and something like four times that of the Benz. Larger and larger engines were developed for different purposes; the bigger ones being, of necessity, fitted with water-cooled cylinder heads.

De Dion tricycles were entered, in the appropriate classes, in races and performed wonders; so, one suspects, did their riders as much 'light pedal assistance' must have been needed in order to maintain the speeds they did. Motor tricycling soon became popular in Paris and even women were to be seen buzzing about on De Dion 'trikes'.

Within a very short time, despite the experts who said that the high speed engines must rattle themselves to pieces in no time, De Dion Bouton engines were being sold in quantity to other firms who used them for bicycles, tricycles and various strange and improbable quadricycles and three wheeled tandem 'forecars' which ante-dated the light car pro-

'L'OBEISSANTE', 1873

Amédée Bollée, senior, built this steam omnibus, *L'Obeissante*, in 1873. It had Ackermann steering, independent suspension and was capable of over 20 m.p.h.

per. This trend continued when the light car appeared on the market. The first De Dion Bouton 4-wheeled rear-engined voiturette was produced late in 1899, with a 3½ h.p. water cooled engine, a most ingenious constant mesh 2-speed gear and unsprung rear live axle. An improved version with a properly sprung back axle and final drive system similar to that of the steam vehicles, followed it in 1900 and was immediately and deservedly successful.

It is impossible now to say how many firms at the turn of the century launched out as motor manufacturers using De Dion Bouton engines as the essential part of their designs. The engines were also widely copied as well as being bought direct from the factory, and the firm suffered a good deal from low grade imitations of their engines and components being passed off as genuine. Louis Renault is among the most famous of the makers who depended upon De Dion Bouton for engines at the start of his career as a motor manufacturer.

It is impossible to describe all the varieties of motor car, good, bad or indifferent, produced in France between 1895 and 1900 but at least one family must be mentioned by name.

The Bollées exercised almost as important an influence on affairs as Panhard-Levassor or De Dion Bouton. The family consisted of Amédée Bollée, *père*, Léon Bollée, his elder son and Amédée, *fils*, all three of whom were designers, whilst a third son, Camille, drove in some of the early races. The elder Bollée produced a number of light steam omnibuses between 1873 and 1885, and he was one of the first engineers to arrange the steering of a mechanical vehicle on the modern system of independently pivoted front wheels, which Ackermann had patented in 1818 on behalf of the inventor, Georg Lenkensperger. The engines and Field-type boilers of Bollée's steamers were not particularly remarkable, but his chassis, steering, transmission and braking details were very well thought out. Some of his early vehicles had independent suspension of all four wheels, and in his 'La Mancelle' series of 1878 he anticipated, with his steam plant, the Panhard-Levassor layout of machinery. Bollée steamers were used in Berlin, a few were built under licence in Germany, and one of these was taken on a demonstration trip to St. Petersburg.

Bollee's 10-steater 'bus, 'La Nouvelle', built in 1880, was the only steamer to cover the course of the Paris-Bordeux-Paris Race in 1895.

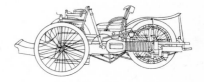

FAMOUS TRICAR

Léon Bollée's tandem tricar, for which he 'invented' the name '*voiturette*', was first produced in December, 1895. It was a noisy and temperamental machine, but capable of more than 30 m.p.h.

It did not do particularly well simply because of one of those maddening mishaps for which no one can be blamed. At one of the routine halts to take on water Bollée *père* found one of the big-end bearings slightly overheated so, in addition to re-charging its oil-cup, he laid a pad of wet rags on top of it. Unfortunately, he then forgot it and when the party moved off the cooling compress was drawn into the machinery with disastrous results. Repairs took a long time and 'La Nouvelle' finally limped on with a bent connecting rod and a broken cross-head guide hastily patched and riveted.

After this Bollée *père* devoted his attention to designing vehicle components rather than vehicles, and some of his patents, such as an hydraulic clutch and a progressively-variable automatic transmission for petrol cars, have a very modern ring. In December 1895, his son Léon displayed one of the most fearsome yet famous of the early motor tricars.

The Léon Bollée tandem tricar was one of those productions which was highly successful in spite of its shortcomings. One of its many peculiarites was that there was no clutch between the engine and the sliding-pinion change speed gear — the first-motion pinions were, indeed, carried on the crankshaft which consequently lived a very hard life. From a pulley on the second motion shaft the power was transmitted to the single back wheel by a flat leather belt, and the wheel itself could be slid to and fro in its forks, by a suitable lever, in order to tighten the belt to make it drive or to slacken it to provide a neutral position. On moving the driving wheel as far forwards as it would go the belt rim was brought to bear on a fixed wooden brake block which, in the fullness of time, brought the contrivance to rest.

The Léon Bollée was noisy, temperamental, exhausting and lovable. The engine was slung low down on the left hand side of the frame, where its air-cooling was impeded by the driver's leg and where the burner for the hot-tube ignition was bound to be choked by dust or swamped by spray from the back wheel. In wet weather the braking power declined from negligible to non-existent, whilst the machine's ability to skid became positively awe inspiring; fortunately, however, as many people have observed, the designer had arranged that the passenger in the front chair should intervene between the driver and the accident. Nevertheless the machine was a great success because its power to weight ratio was

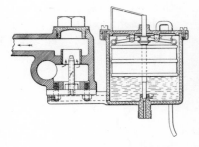

MAYBACH CARBURETTOR, 1893

Maybach float-feed spray carburettor; patented 1893. Maybach's device was the ancestor of the modern spray carburettor. There was only one jet and the inventor claimed that as the level of fuel in it was always kept constant by the float and needle-valve, the mixture strength would remain constant despite variations in engine speed: this was soon found to be too optimistic.

good, and when it could be persuaded to go at all it went like a dose of salts. It was, for a time, the fastest vehicle on sale to the public being capable of a good 30 m.p.h.: an English version was sold as the 'Coventry Motette' and the first motor tricar Herbert Austin designed for the Wolseley Company was clearly inspired by the Léon Bollée.

By the end of the century when his tricar declined in popularity Léon Bollée had designed a four-wheeled car which was built under licence by Darracq, whilst his brother Amédée had designed a motor car for the great De Dietrich industrial complex in Alsace-Lorraine. The Bollées were thus indirectly responsible for launching two of the most successful motor car concerns, although their designs were soon supplanted by others. The Amédée Bollée racing cars, known from their rudimentary streamlining as *torpilleurs*, had rear-mounted 4-cylinder horizontal engines with twin carburettors and independent front wheel suspension.

Although a great deal was going on in other parts of the world, only France could justly claim to have a really thriving motor industry before

YOU CAN BELIEVE ANYTHING IF YOU TRY

E. J. Pennington came to England from America in 1896 and sold his almost worthless designs to the Lawson syndicate for £. 100,000. In this advertisement it is claimed that a Pennington motor bicycle got up enough speed to jump over a 65 foot wide river.

the twentieth century. On paper, industries existed in England and America but in reality these were shadowy affairs by comparison. Even in Germany the bulk of the trade was in Benz's hands (he sold over 600 cars in 1899) with Daimler and the rest barely scratching the surface: the Daimler engine business was thriving, it is true, but it is very doubtful if the motor car division showed a profit.

In March of 1890 Daimler yielded to the persuasion of his friend Max Duttenhofer and enlarged his business in preparation for making it, in the following November, into a public company. One of the specific objects of the new Daimler Motoren Gesellschaft was to make and sell horseless vehicles, but almost before the ink was dry on the Articles of Association Daimler quarrelled with his new directors, resigned from the Board and retired with Wilhelm Maybach to set up an independent business as consulting engineer.

The first Daimler motor cars to be produced in series and sold to the public were, in consequence of this breach, designed by one Georg Schrödter who took as his model, obviously, Daimler's second experimental belt-driven carriage of 1889. With modifications and improvements these rear-engined, belt-driven Daimlers remained in production until 1900: they retained the curiously archaic system of steering by a centre pivoted axle but as their maximum speed was only about 15 m.p.h. this worked well enough. Though slow and old-fashioned even by 1895 standards, these cars sold fairly well because, like their Benz contemporaries, they were simple, relatively quiet and very reliable. Many were fitted with ponderous brougham or landaulet bodies.

In 1895 the Daimler directors realised they were being outdistanced by the French; the quarrel with Daimler was composed, he and Maybach returned to the company and under their joint direction more modern designs were put in hand alongside the belt driven car. Both private car and lorry chassis were produced, and in the former the Panhard-Levassor influence is very strong in the general layout. Two notable Daimler features were evolved during this period. These were the selective or 'gate' gear control (a marked improvement on Levassor's progressive or 'run-through' system) and the famous 'honeycomb' radiator, both of which are generally, but wrongly, held to have seen the light of day for the first time on the Mercedes model of 1900. In 1899 some of

FAMOUS TRICYCLE

A De Dion Bouton tricycle of 1896: this was the type of machine which brought Georges Bouton's efficient high speed motor to the fore.

the Daimler cars were equipped with the new Simms-Bosch low-tension magneto ignition in place of the hot tubes.

Having adopted the Panhard-Levassor formula, in essentials, the Daimler concern went the whole hog in 1899 and produced the 'Phoenix' Daimler racing car with a four cylinder engine, rated at 24 h.p. (P. S. rating), with a capacity of 5½ litres which was considerably larger and more powerful than anything the French had done. The car was capable of some 50 m.p.h. but unfortunately its handling quantities did not match its speed and, at the request of Emile Jellinek (a customer, turned unofficial agent and finally sales director of Daimler), Maybach re-designed it so that it re-appeared, a few weeks after Daimler's death, as the 35 h.p. Mercedes* which set a new standard in automobile design and performance.

By this time the motor industry in Germany had made great strides, but it must be said that many of the manufacturers, as in other countries, contributed nothing new at first but contented themselves with building French cars under licence. Prominent amongst them were the Opel brothers who adopted the Darracq design, Dixi who copied Decauville and Adler and others who followed De Dion Bouton.

The American motor industry in the 1890's seems curiously backward when one considers the wealth and industrial resources of the country, but this apparent lack of initiative is less curious when it is remembered that outside the towns most American roads became almost impassable in bad weather. Once the motor car 'caught on' the Americans set about improving their highways with characteristic energy (though even today their minor roads are far worse than English ones), but it is no exaggeration to say that, at first, American inventors and pioneers were as effectively stifled by lack of good roads as their English counterparts were by restrictive legislation.

It ill becomes an Englishman to state positively who was the first American to make a petrol-engined motor car, as American experts themselves are unable to agree on this point. At one time the date of 1891 was claimed on behalf of Henry Ford (a mistake which is still often quoted), but it is clear that his first crude experimental machine was built in 1896. Haynes and Duryea are rival contenders, the former claiming 1894 as his *annus mirabilis*, whilst 1892, or 1893 are claimed on behalf

SERPOLLET'S DRIVER'S LICENCE
Driver's licence issued to Léon Serpollet in 1889, 16th of August.

* The name of Jellinek's eldest daughter given, at his suggestion, to the new model to overcome the understandable dislike the French had for anything German.

of the Duryea brothers who, in their later years, were estranged and put forward opposing claims. Recent evidence shows that a photographer called Walter Lewis swore an affidavit in 1927 to the effect that he photographed a 3-wheeled 'gas-buggy' in March 1891 on behalf of its inventor Mr Lambert. This evidence, having been tendered 36 years after the alleged event, should not be accepted as conclusive, and in any case Lambert does not appear to have followed up his initial attempt but to have joined the ranks of those who made one or two experiments which led nowhere. It does seem fairly certain that the first commercial company to be founded in the U.S.A., expressly to make petrol cars, was the Duryea Motor Waggon Co.: the date was 1895.

Duryea 'won' the first officially recognised American motor race which was organised by the 'Times-Herald' newspaper in November 1895. The victory was far from resounding, as the Duryea took some nine hours to cover the 54 mile course, but the only other competitor to finish was a Benz, imported and modified by Müller of New York, which needed so much manual help over the slushy roads that the driver collapsed from sheer exhaustion.

Most of the early American efforts were based upon a slow-running horizontal engine with primary drive and change-speed gear by belts and pulleys in the Benz manner. As American designers remained wholly oblivious to the information and experience gained in other lands their plagiarism was unintentional. By the beginning of the new century the typical American motor car, as executed by such masters as Olds, Winton, Packard and Ford, still relied upon a large, inefficient, slow-running horizontal engine, usually with one cylinder but occasionally with two, but the belt drive had been abandoned in favour of a 2-speed and reverse epicyclic gear system mounted on an extension of the crankshaft and driving the rear live axle by a central chain. Steam and electric runabouts on the same general plan were also popular for a number of years. The petrol-engined cars of this type, of which the 'curved dash' Oldsmobile (Page 81) is a typical example, were deservedly popular but of rather limited performance.

Some European cars were, of course, imported quite early and the Steinway Piano Company had been licensees of the Daimler patents since 1891, but the 'gas-buggy' type of runabout remained in production

DURYEA, 1893/4
Duryea's first experimental car of 1893/4 was not a success. An improved 4-wheel version followed.

alongside 'conventional' vertical-engined European-style cars which the leading manufacturers soon began to copy, improve and generally adapt to native requirements. Before 1914, therefore, one can trace European ancestry in many of the most important American makes; the Pierce, for instance, derived from De Dion Bouton, the vertical-engined Packards differed little from the Mors on which they were based, the Simplex had much in common with Mercedes and the Thomas was inspired by Berliet. As time went on the American designers developed their own distinctive notions and made their own contribution to automobile history, which is dealt with in Chapter 7.

If the American industry lagged surprisingly behind France, English backwardness was positively disgraceful when one considers that the supremacy of Britain in the last century was based upon the native inventiveness and industrial enterprise. There was little point in devoting time and money to developing motor cars in Great Britain when motoring was, in effect, illegal. Since the Acts of 1861 and 1865 (slightly modified by another of 1878), the only commercial outlet for native inventiveness had been in the field of the heavy steam traction engine which could operate profitably within the limitations of the 4 m.p.h. speed restriction.

By the 1890's a few influential men became attracted to the new locomotion, as a hobby or sport at first, and soon realised that Great Britain would be left behind in the new industry unless the law was altered. Men of the calibre of the Hon. Evelyn Ellis and Sir David Salomons bought cars in France, shipped them to England and began to organise support for a change in the laws.

With the feeling in the air that something might one day be done to improve matters, a handful of business men and engineers turned their attention to the motor vehicle and a few experimental cars were constructed; most of these, like the Bremer which survives, were so crude that their inventors did not pursue the matter further once they realised how far the Continental manufacturers had advanced.

Typical of these pioneer efforts was the little belt-driven machine built by J. H. Knight as a 3-wheeler in 1895 and subsequently altered into a 4-wheeler. This little car went reasonably well, and had a top speed of about 8 m.p.h., but Mr Knight, as a practising engineer, could see that the Benz cars which could be bought in London from 1896 onwards

WINTON, 1895/6
Alexander Winton's first car, 1895/6 Winton was one of the foremost makes in America in the early years of motoring.

were much superior to his own, which was accordingly laid aside whilst its designer became a firm advocate of the Benz.

On behalf of the Wolseley Sheep-Shearing Machine Company. Herbert Austin designed a tricar in 1896 (the claimed date of 1895 cannot be substantiated) which had many points of similarity to the Léon Bollée, but no 4-wheeled Wolesley design materialised until mid-1899 and nothing was available for sale until 1901.

The only undeniably native design of this first period, and the first full-scale, 4-wheeled, English, petrol car, to be followed by commercial production in due course, was the Lanchester (Page 42) which was designed by Fredrick Lanchester and built, with the help of his brother George, in 1894/5. The first road test was made in February 1896, and a new and wholly unconventional vibrationless 2-cylinder, double crankshaft engine was installed soon after. Two more experimental Lanchesters were made in 1897/8 and the production model, which was developed from them in 1900, was a most brilliant achievement technically but so far in advance of its time in many respects that few people could understand it.

In 1896 two important things happened: firstly the efforts of the small band of enthusiasts bore fruit, and the Locomotives on Highways Act was passed and came into force on November 14th. The Government gave grudging recognition to the dawn of a new age by abolishing the need for a man to walk ahead of each mechanical vehicle to give warning, and by raising the speed limit from the derisory 4 m.p.h. to an over-cautious 12 m.p.h. The second significant happening was the appearance of a company promoter called Lawson who organised a celebration of this relative freedom by collecting together all the motor cars he could and arranging an 'Emancipation Run' from London to Brighton.

Organized is not, perhaps, the right word for this first 'Brighton Run' wavered, as did so many of Lawson's affairs, between farce and chaos.

Lawson was a fairly unscrupulous financial juggler, who was also an exceptionally far sighted man with some knowledge of industrial management. He had made a fortune out of company promoting during the bicycle boom and he saw, as few people did, that the motor industry was going to be big business one day. Even before the Act of 1896 was drafted Mr Lawson set about making sure that no matter who lost

WOLSELEY, 1904

A 1904 single-cylinder 6 h.p. Wolseley with horizontal engine. The contemporary 'Little Siddeley' was exactly the same except for a different bonnet and radiator and was made in the same factory.

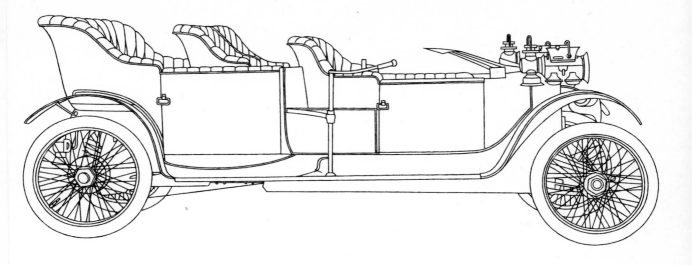

money when motoring became legal, he was going to profit. And profit he did, personally, even though none of his motor companies survived for long without loosing the shareholders a lot of money. Lawson planned to control the unborn motor industry, to which end, in collaboration with the notorious Martin Rucker and Ernest Hooley (who subsequently went to prison for fraud) he set up the British Motor Syndicate to buy and exploit every motor patent, valuable or worthless, that could be bought.

The first move in the Lawson game was to buy the Daimler patent rights from Frederick Simms, the English licensee, for £. 35,000. The Syndicate then set up the Daimler Motor Company in Coventry, appointed themselves as directors together with some nominees, raised a lot of capital and bought the Daimler rights from themselves at a profit. This pattern was repeated *ad nauseam*. Patents were bought, usually at an inflated price the better to impress would-be investors, whether they had any merit or not, by the Syndicate which then sold or hired the right to manufacture under those patents to manufacturing companies bought or set up for the purpose.

LANCHESTER, 1906

1906, 28 h.p. 6-cylinder Lanchester. The Lanchester arrangement of 1905 onwards with the engine placed between driver and front passenger made it possible to provide plenty of space on a relatively short chassis with all seats within the wheelbase. Like all Lanchester models this car has 3-speed epicyclic gears, with pre-selector control, worm-gear live axle and cantilever suspension front and back.

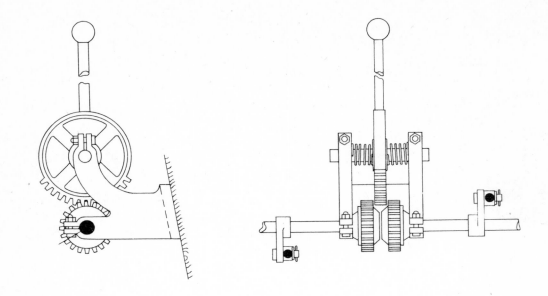

The fact that many of the patents were of dubious validity, and many of the proposed designs (such as the Pennington for which £. 100,000 was paid) were quite worthless, mattered not at all to the Lawson gang. They drew their fees and commission on formation of each new company, plus their directorial salaries from each Board and in addition shared in the profit the original syndicate made from selling or hiring-out manufacturing rights. It was a cosy little set up for a number of years, and when any company got into financial difficulties, or the share-holders grew restless, it was easy enough to go into liquidation and start again. In this way the grandiose Great Horseless Carriage Company became the Motor Manufacturing Company, and the Daimler concern was reformed more than once at great loss to the shareholders. Consequently by the end of the century the financial world had no confidence left in *any* motor manufacturing proposal.

In addition to their blatant share pushing the Syndicate claimed the right to royalty payment on every car made by firms outside their own organisation, threatened buyers of 'unlicenced' cars with prosecution and even demanded royalties on cars and components imported into the

DAIMLER'S CHANGE-SPEED CONTROL, 1894

The change-speed control of the belt-driven Daimler cars of 1894 onwards. The 'gear' lever moves both sideways and to-and-fro to select each of the four speeds, thus anticipating the 'gate' or 'H-slot' gear shift.

country. These actions, or the threat of them, were enough to frighten off a number of would-be designers, business men or prospective customers. The English pioneers, having been stifled for a generation by governmental grandmotherliness, now found themselves in a Lawsonian sea full of financial sharks.

If one were to believe the publicity, a thriving motor industry had been brought into being, under Lawson's beneficent auspices, at a stroke of the wand even before the passage of the Emancipation Act. The English Daimler Co., the Great Horseless Carriage Co., The Coventry Motor Co., The Beeston Cycle and Motor Co., and others advertised every conceivable (and many inconceivable) variety of motor bicycle, tricycle, quadricycle, light car, heavy car, omnibus or lorry, but any customer trying to buy one in 1896 would have been put off with promises and excuses. A few 'English' Daimlers were sold, it is true, late in that year but they were in reality Cannstatt-Daimlers disguised with English name plates; when the company did start producing, in very limited numbers, in 1897, their models were more-or-less direct copies of Panhard-Levassor designs and some were confusingly described as 'Parisian Daimlers'.

The chicanery and ramifications of Lawson's 'motor empire' which did not finally collapse until 1903, would provide material for several books. Enough has been said to show that he hindered rather than helped to establish a sound motor industry. There were, of course, independent individuals or companies who carried on business, chiefly by importing or copying established designs, either in defiance of Lawson or by knuckling under and paying royalties. One of Lawson's early moves had been to start the Motor Car Club, the members of which soon realised it was no more than a trading organisation chiefly concerned to puff Mr Lawson's schemes. A break-away movement under Simms and Harrington-Moore in 1897 resulted in the foundation of the Automobile Club of Great Britain and Ireland (now the Royal Automobile Club), and English motorists and manufacturers at last had a respectable organisation to look after their interests.

Between 1897 and 1900 the number of cars in use in Great Britain steadily increased in spite of public derision, the fulminations of the carriage-gentry and police persecution. Many of the motor cars sold by

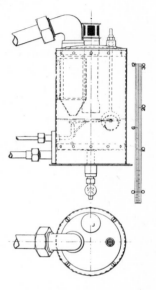

THE BENZ CARBURETTOR

Benz's design for a surface carburettor, taken from his patent specification drawing. The carburettors actually used on the Benz cars from 1885 to 1901 differed in detail but were similar in principle. The air drawn into the engine passed over the surface of the fuel in the carburettor and consequently 'licked up' petrol vapour from it. Given sufficiently volatile fuel these carburettors worked well but were rather bulky.

the increasing band of dealers and agents were described as 'All-British' and some of them were actually made in England; but in nearly every case their ancestry could be traced to the Continent. Thus the Triumph was really a Renault, the New Orleans was a Vivinus from Belgium whilst Arnold, International, Star and Liver all drew their inspiration from Benz. The Marshall, to make things even more difficult, was an English copy of the Hurtu which was a French variant on the Benz theme.

The great motoring event of 1900 was the 1,000 Miles Trial organised by the Automobile Club. Here the true picture is revealed, for although more than half of the thirty four different makes represented were described as all-British, only two of the 4-wheeled passenger cars were of undoubted native ancestry. These were the Lanchester and the Wolseley. Even the Napier, so soon to become the best known English make, was still so similar to the Panhard-Levassor that one description of it ran: 'Napier's Panhard-Levassor-Daimler carriage with Napier engine.' At least, however, the Trial convincingly showed the public that the motor car was more than just a rich man's plaything, and the tiny motor industry could look forward to the twentieth century with confidence.

MORS, 1904
1904 24 h.p. 4-cylinder Mors; an impressive touring car capable of 50 m.p.h.

As we have seen many of the very early motor cars were surprisingly reliable, and this seems incompatible with the common picture of the pioneer motorist as a man who spent more time stranded by the roadside, struggling with recalcitrant machinery, than he did bowling along in a cloud of dust with pigs, hens, dogs and old women flying in terror before him.

The explanation of the anomaly is twofold. Firstly the Benzs, Panhards, Cannstatt-Daimlers and so forth of the 1890's were built by rule of thumb with fairly generous, even over-generous, margins of strength and yet were propelled by engines so feeble that most of the mechanical parts were but lightly stressed. The second, and more important, reason is that an early Panhard-Levassor might be wonderfully well behaved in the hands of Emile Levassor or Hippolyte Panhard but a perfect beast in the hands of Mr Snooks. In other words the constant roadside breakdowns which gave the horse-and-carriage gentry such hearty laughs, were mostly trivial affairs which an experienced motorist (had such a person existed) could have diagnosed and cured without much difficulty.

There were, of course, serious mechanical failures occasionally even in the best of cars, and some of the many machines which came on the market were so ineptly designed that they were bound to give trouble, but in general the difficulties arose because few ordinary members of the public were acquainted with any machine more complicated than a bicycle. Consequently any trivial mishap like a loose terminal, an inlet valve stuck open (a common fault), or a carburettor choked with dirt from the dusty roads could leave them stranded; and if these and similar troubles did not bring them to a standstill then, inevitably, tyre failures would.

It might be supposed that the first manufacturers would have taken pains to give their customers clear directions on how to drive and care for so novel a device. They did no such thing; with a few honourable exceptions makers' handbooks have always been so badly written as to be almost useless, and in the early days few manufacturers issued any instructions at all. So the hapless buyer, who quite possibly thought you merely took your seat, pressed a button and let the machine do all the rest, found himself confronted with a mystifying array of machinery and a variety of levers, knobs, handles and pedals which sometimes seem to suggest the early car makers thought human beings were equipped with the arms of an octopus, the legs of a centipede and the dexterity of a conjourer.

At the beginning of the century a number of little firms tried to cash in on the motor boom and the cars they made, generally in the single-cylinder voiturette class, by the simple process of buying proprietory components, mostly from France, and assembling them in backyard workshops with few facilities, were often pretty bad. Some of these confections were, indeed, horrible both in design and execution, but the better firms were already turning out well-designed and finished machines which were capable of giving good service. Even the best of them, however, needed sympathetic handling and a degree of constant care and adjustment which would seem excessive by modern standards. It was exceptional, for instance, in 1900 to motor a thousand miles without having to grind-in valves, and the prudent motorist soon learnt to adjust his brakes every time he took his car out. Let us look at the evolution of design which gradually made this constant tinkering less necessary.

Engine design soon became fairly stereotyped. The original Benz arrangement of a modified gas-engine with exposed crank and connecting rod was obsolete by 1901, but until well on in the century many manufacturers, particularly in America, favoured the horizontal engine and such famous firms as Olds, Ford, Cadillac, Wolseley and many more made their reputations with horizontal-engined cars. The most usual form of horizontal engine was fairly slow running and was arranged with its crankshaft parallel with the axles. Most had one cylinder, some had two (side by side or horizontally opposed), but there were a few 4-cylinder horizontal engines and one or two with eight cylinders—though most of these, such as the Buffum, were freaks which did not succeed.

By 1901, however, it was clear that the easiest line of development for large and medium sized cars was that which Panhard et Levassor had laid down, even though the *système Panhard* did not necessarily provide so elegant or technically superior an arrangement as, for example, the Lanchester with its ingenious horizontally opposed, 2-cylinder, double crankshaft, vibrationless engine. By 1904 or thereabouts it began to be apparent also, that even in the *voiturette* field the big car style was bound to prevail, and the vertical engine mounted under a bonnet became so *de rigeur* that those makers who continued, often for good reason, to use a horizontal engine in the centre of their chassis had to fit their cars with dummy bonnets.

When Levassor first used the Phoenix engine, with its two cylinders in line instead of in a V formation, the next step was obvious—when more power was wanted more cylinders were added. Four cylinder engines first appeared in 1896 but they were still uncommon for any but outright racing cars before 1900. The constructional difficulties of making long multi-throw crankshafts satisfactorily were considerable, and the next logical step, the six-cylinder-in-line engine, first made a commercial success by Napier from 1903 onwards, posed a new problem in the shape of torsional crankshaft vibration. This difficulty was avoided by Lanchester who made his first 6-cylinder model of 1905 with an 'oversquare' engine with a stroke of only three inches and a bore of four inches. To solve a difficulty for the Daimler Company, whose first 6-cylinder model was unsaleable because of the crankshaft vibration, Dr. Lanchester invented the torsional vibration damper (known in America as the Warner Damper, the manufacturing rights having been sold to the Warner Company) in 1909, and this made a big contribution to the development of the 6-cylinder engine.

During the early period therefore a general rule of thumb was that small cars of up to 10 or 12 h.p. had single- or twin-cylinder engines, and in the range from 12 to 24 h.p. or so four cylinders were generally used. There were also, in the luxury class, a number of models of 60, 80 or even more horsepower made with giant 4-cylinder engines, but from about 1909 the six-in-line was favoured for cars of about 30 h.p. or over. As the specific output rose only (on average) from some 4 h.p. per litre to about 10 h.p. per litre between 1900 and 1910 it will be seen that these engines were very large by modern standards: the 12 h.p. Panhard of 1901 for example had an engine capacity of four litres from which the modern designer would expect some 200 h.p.

There was also a vogue for three cylinder engines, of about 10-18 h.p., which lasted roughly from 1904 to 1907.

The use of 4-cylinder engines for the smallest and lightest type of conventional car was one of the innovations which originated largely in Germany. From about 1908 onwards, when English and French cars in the 8-10 h.p. range were almost invariably twin-cylindered (some, indeed, still had single cylinder engines), and when American design in general

RENAULT, 1904

1904 Renault with 4-cylinder (90 × 120 mm) engine developing about 20 h.p.. The Renault-style dashboard-mounted radiator made the engine very accessible and avoided road dust being drawn into the bonnet. Many other manufacturers copied the arrangement. The domed mudguards on this car were fitted about 1920.

68

was concerned with cars of 20 h.p. or more, nearly all the leading German firms brought out light cars with excellent 4-cylinder engines, some with overhead valves, in the range of 850-1,200 c.c. This brought to the light-car customer a degree of smoothness and silence hitherto reserved for the big-car owner.

One of the principal contributors to this trend was Ettore Bugatti, although his productions were only 'German' by reason of the fact that his workshops were in Alsace which the Germans had wrested from France after the Franco-Prussian war. Bugatti not only made his mark with his own exquisitely made 4- and 8-cylinder cars but with his designs for other firms, and in 1912 his T-head 4-cylinder engine of 55 mm x 90 mm for the Bébé Peugeot was thought too small to be practical, but nevertheless it helped pave the way towards making the 2-cylinder car a back number.

The cylinders were at first generally cast singly or in pairs; blocks of four cylinders or more were rare before 1907 and uncommon before 1912. As foundry techniques improved it began to be possible for designers to give greater rigidity to their engines (an important factor in giving smoothness of running and longevity to the crankshaft and its bearings) by using 'monobloc' cylinder castings. Although the home market for cars in Belgium was small, some very fine motor cars were evolved there, and the ironworks in the Liège district became famous for cylinder castings which were exported to manufacturers in France, Germany and Great Britain.

In a rather similar way Sweden made her mark on the motor industry by becoming, for some years, the most important supplier of ball-bearings to the manufacturers of Europe and Great Britain. Sweden herself had virtually no motor industry, her tiny output of private cars being confined to the rival firms of Scania and Vabis who amalgamated in 1911.

A feature of early engines which would strike the modern eye was that so many of their entrails were exposed. Copper pipes for oil, water and carburettor writhe about in labyrinthine confusion. Timing-gears, cams, tappets and valve springs were all laid bare to the eye and vulnerable to dust. By 1903 or so the gear wheels to drive the camshafts were generally encased and properly lubricated, but exposed valve tappets and springs were still quite common as late as 1914.

DAIMLER 'SIAMESE', 1898

English Daimler, 1898, with 'Siamese' or Double Phaeton body. The 2-cylinder engine and chassis were very similar to the contemporary Panhard-Levassor.

From the earliest period the exhaust valves were much as they are to-day, except that heat resisting steels had not been developed, but the inlet valves, instead of being positively opened by cam and tappet mechanism, were opened merely by atmospheric pressure when the piston descended on the intake stroke and caused a vacuum in the cylinder. These were called 'automatic' or 'atmospheric' inlet valves and, obviously, as they depended on 'suction' to open them they could only be furnished with very weak springs, usually made adjustable, to close them (on compression and firing strokes the pressure in the cylinder held them shut) and they were in consequence a frequent source of trouble: too tight a spring would delay opening and cause loss of power, and too slack a spring would allow the valve to bounce on its seat and ultimately break. Also, burnt oil or soot on the valve stem would be enough to make it stick.

Another disadvantage was that an 'automatic' valve could not be held open beyond the end of the intake stroke in order to take advantage of the inertia of the gases in the induction pipe to help fill the cylinder as full as possible; also an automatic valve tends to behave properly at only one speed consequently the use of such valves, together with the shortcomings of early carburettors and ignition systems, tended to make the engines very inflexible. As, however, all the early car designers were influenced by gas-engine practice and tried to keep engine speed constant in the interest of fuel economy, varying car speed by changing gear, the retention of the gas-engine type of inlet valve was understandable enough. It must be said, too, that the automatic inlet valve worked quite well at the low speeds of the early years; as improved designs and materials allowed speeds to be increased above 1,500 r.p.m. the inadequacy of the automatic valve became more apparent and it fell into disfavour from about 1903 onwards.

The automatic inlet valves had usually been inverted over the exhaust valves, both working in pockets at the side of the combustion spaces. With the adoption of mechanical inlet valves, worked positively by cam and tappet like the exhaust valves, it became common practice to arrange the inlet valve, or valves, on one side of the engine and the exhausts opposite. This arrangement was known as the T-head and despite the theoretically bad shape of the combustion chamber which resulted, and

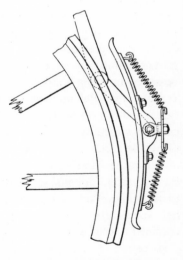

PRICE'S BRAKE SHOE

Price's patent brake shoe, fitted as an optional extra to some of the Benz cars in England. These patent shoes were less apt to damage the tyres than the little 'spoon' brakes supplied by Benz.

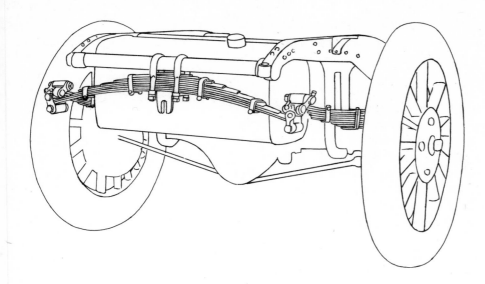

the need for two camshafts, it gave reasonably smooth combustion as long as compression ratios were not much higher than 4 : 1. In order to make do with only one set of cams, and to simplify things generally, the L-head arrangement, with all valves on one side of the engine, became common from about 1906 onwards and remained supreme for all but high performance engines for some thirty years. Overhead valves, which allow better combustion chamber shapes, *were* used by many manufacturers but, in general, were not thought suitable for any but sporting machinery before 1914.

Other varieties of valve were tried such as rotary valves, cuff valves, split-ring valves and so forth but the only system to become at all popular, apart from the conventional poppet valve arrangement, was the sleeve valve. The double-sleeve valve, invented by C. Y. Knight, an American, was developed by the English Daimler Co. and used by them, and by Panhard-Levassor, Minerva and some others, for many years. It had the advantages of giving good port area, good combustion space and mechanical silence against the disadvantages of complication, expense and the need for such copious lubrication that a sleeve valve car

SPRING ARRANGEMENT
This combination of longitudinal and transverse springs was popular in the early days. It was sometimes called 'platform suspension'.

could always be distinguished by the thick cloud of oily exhaust smoke it emitted. The single-sleeve valve gear, devised by Burt and Mc Cullum and used by Argyll, was more efficient, but made more contribution to the aero-engine than the motor car.

Mention has already been made of the reluctance the earliest motor engines showed to run over a wide range of speed, as modern ones do. This made constant gear changing a necessity and, at the same time, more difficult. The trouble arose in part from the designers' reluctance to break away from gas-engine practice which was based upon the fact that the best fuel efficiency was to be had at optimum speed only. The other factor was that early design features, such as the automatic inlet valves, did not lend themselves readily towards functioning at different speeds. The present day driver would be nonplused to find no throttle pedal with which to control engine and car speed, but before about 1903 many carburettors had no throttle valves and the accelerator pedal found on a few makes, or its equivalent hand lever, was concerned only to over-ride the mechanical governor which normally prevented the engine running too fast. This gave nothing like the sensitivity of control we now take for granted.

The reason for this was that the majority of early carburettors could provide a correctly proportioned mixture at one rate of gas-flow only, and any attempt at charge-volume throttling would have altered the strength of the mixture. The surface carburettors used by Benz and some other pioneers *could* respond fairly well to throttling, but in these the inflammable mixture was formed by passing the air on its way to the engine over the surface of the fuel in a suitable vessel. Baffle plates, perforated pipes and other devices were arranged to help direct the air over the surface, and these simple vapourisers were satisfactory enough, but they were very bulky and were apt to vapourise the lighter elements of the fuel and leave behind a heavier residue which gradually interfered with the proper action.

Something better was needed, and in 1893 Wilhelm Maybach, Daimler's assistant, patented a float-feed spraying carburettor which is the ancestor of all modern instruments; this was immediately used on the Daimler and Panhard engines and was quickly copied, with slight variations, by other manufacturers.

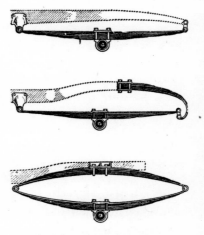

DIFFERENT TYPES OF SUSPENSION SPRING

The semi- or half-elliptic spring: the most usual type. The three-quarter-elliptic spring: popular for rear suspension, and the full-elliptic spring, not much used after 1900.

These first spray carburettors were very simple, with only one jet and some arrangement whereby the amount of air entering the intake could be controlled. In his patent specification Maybach claimed that the float-feed kept the level of fuel absolutely constant in the jet and that in consequence the proportions of fuel and air would remain automatically constant at all speeds of gas-flow. Alas: as the fuel was not vapourised but carried forward in the form of a fine mist of droplets, Herr Maybach was too optimistic as the laws governing the different behaviour of gases and liquids could not be so readily bent at his behest.

The Maybach carburettor, and its contemporaries, could not, therefore, be furnished with throttles and they worked well only because the speed range of the engines to which they were fitted was so small. As soon as car manufacturers and drivers began to appreciate the advantage of having a throttle as the principal means of engine control, in the steam engine fashion, an intensive period of experiment was started to improve the spray carburettor.

The first step was to provide an extra-air inlet, under the driver's control by a suitable lever on steering column or dashboard, so that mixture strength could be readily adjusted while the car was moving. Attempts to make this an automatic function soon followed and Commandant Krebs, a director of Panhard et Levassor, brought out one of the first 'automatic' carburettors in 1898. This depended on the vacuum in the inlet tract acting upon a spring-loaded valve so as to admit more or less air according to engine speed. This was a step in the right direction but the Krebs carburettor, and its contemporaries and successors, still needed cooperation from the driver with his hand control if really good results were to be obtained.

The search for the truly automatic carburettor in the first years of the century seemed as hopeless as the quest for the holy grail, and led one motorist to say that the automatic carburettor did no more than automatically give the wrong mixture at every engine speed. Most manufacturers made their own carburettors, and the era of the proprietory instrument did not start until about 1906. The ideas varied from the merely weird to the outright improbable; some were complex, like the Napier hydraulic air-inlet control, some were brilliantly simple like the Lanchester wick carburettor and amongst the most satisfactory were

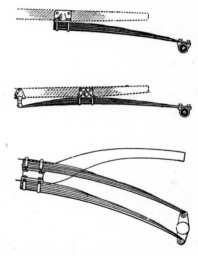

DIFFERENT TYPES OF SUSPENSION SPRING

A popular form of suspension was the quarter-elliptic. The cantilever spring was originally used by Lanchester but by 1912 quite often used on luxury cars. The double-quarter-elliptic spring was not often seen, but provided 'parallel motion' without the expense of radius links.

the ingenious carburettors found on some of the early single cylinder American runabouts: these, admittedly, had only a fairly low-speed engine to deal with. The Krebs idea was widely copied, and one of the finest of all early carburettors (and one which was in use with little alteration for some thirty years), the Rolls-Royce, was based on the Krebs principle.

It has often been implied that Gottlieb Daimler showed curious lack of *nous* in persisting with his hot-tube ignition when electric ignition was already quite well known in the gas engine world; but he had two very good reasons for doing so. He wanted his engines to be completely self-contained, which they could not be if the ignition depended upon batteries which must be charged from some source of electric supply current; also the advantages of electric ignition, in his view, were offset by the extreme unreliability of the batteries and coils of seventy-odd years ago, and of the general ignorance of all things worked by electricity which the public at large regarded with awe and apprehension.

Daimler's hot-tube ignition was agreeably simple. A small platinum tube, closed at its outer end, was screwed horizontally into the cylinder head or valve pocket so that the gases would be forced into it on the compression stroke. The exposed, closed, end of the tube was kept at bright-red heat by a suitable petrol-fed burner, the whole business being enclosed in a kind of miniature oven, and as the compressed gas reached the hottest part of the tube it took fire. The residue of burnt gas left in the little tube prevented the next incoming charge from igniting until maximum compression had been reached, and the system was in consequence self timing.

Provided the tube, or tubes, were kept at the correct heat the system was as reliable as it was simple and the ailments from which it suffered— leaking tubes or joints, faulty burners, too much heat causing pre-ignition and backfiring, too little heat causing misfiring, burners blowing out in a cross wind or blowing up in a collision — were such as the veriest amateur could diagnose.

Apart from the fire hazard, the disadvantage of hot-tube ignition for motor car work was that the time of firing, in relation to the position of the piston in the cylinder, could not easily be varied and therefore the timing could not be varied to suit different speeds, and this made another important influence restricting the flexibility of early engines. By

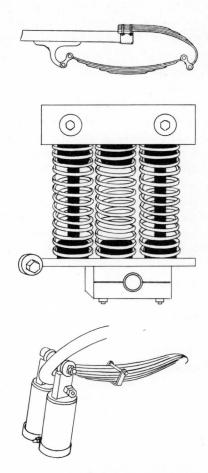

MORE SUSPENSION SPRINGS

A form of three-quarter-elliptic spring for heavy cars, an early arrangement of helical springing c. 1899, and a supplementary spring shackle or shock absorber used with a half-elliptic spring.

1900, hot tube ignition was virtually obsolete, though some firms, such as Panhard-Levassor and (English) Daimler continued to fit tubes as a standby to their electric systems.

The electric apparatus used by Lenoir on his 1860 engine had consisted of a couple of primary cells, a rotating switch, or contact maker, two sparking plugs (Lenoir's engine was 'double-acting' in steam engine fashion, and consequently had a sparking plug at each end of the cylinder; impulses being given on alternate sides of the piston) and a 'trembler' coil — that is an induction coil depending upon an electro-magnetic vibrator to rupture the primary circuit and induce the high tension current in the secondary windings. This was the type of ignition system used by Benz and many others, with such variations as their ingenuity dictated and with the substitution of accumulators for the primary cells.

The combination of rotary switch, or 'wipe contact maker', in the primary circuit and electro-trembler coil worked well enough, though about 2,000 r.p.m. was its limit; subject to the difficulties of making reliable sparking plugs; of insulating the high voltage currents; of getting batteries charged and the deep ignorance of all things electrical on the part of the public. It is hardly surprising that, at first, many manufacturers and their customers preferred the predictable misbehaviour of tube ignition to the wholly unpredictable electricity, the vagaries of which had been admirably summed up by Lord Grimthorpe who wrote of experimental electric clocks in the 1860's and ended his dissertation with: '. . . but remember, sometimes, for no apparent reason, the electric fluid entirely fails to flow. '

As applied to single-cylinder engines, the wiring of the trembler coil system could hardly have been simpler, and it was adapted to multi-cylinder engines by the expedient of adding another contact piece and trembler coil for each additional cylinder. In other words, no distributor was needed for the high tension currents. As each trembler had its own characteristic and rate of vibration, any one cylinder might receive a slightly weaker, and therefore 'later' spark than its neighbour: this led to rough running and loss of power. Napier, Lodge, Winton and Renault led the way in developing high tension distributors which made it possible to supply all the sparking plugs from one coil. On some cars, Napier and early Rolls-Royce for instance, the distributor was placed

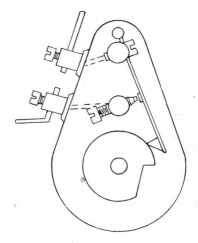

DE DION CONTACT BREAKER, 1895

De Dion Bouton contact breaker. Designed by Georges Bouton in 1895 for his high speed engine and the direct ancestor of the modern type.

in a handsome glass fronted mahogany box on the dashboard where driver and passengers, for no very clear reason, could watch it at work. Although he avoided the battery nuisance by using a magneto generator to supply the low tension current, Henry Ford perpetuated the old fashioned arrangement of a separate trembler coil for each cylinder on his famous Model T and consequently some fifteen million owners, in nineteen years, had to grapple with the vagaries of the multi-coil system.

As early as 1895 Georges Bouton had devised an electric ignition system for his high speed engine which avoided the weaknesses of the trembler coil. He used a modern type of non-trembling coil and a mechanical 'make and break' with a contact blade operated by a cam. This vibrated at low engine speeds to give a succession of sparks at each contact, but at higher speeds functioned much as a modern contact breaker does. Indeed, the modern system of coil ignition is directly descended from Bouton's arrangement, which functioned splendidly but was cursed by many as the contact breaker needed rather frequent and delicate adjustment. In order to make everything as reliable as possible De Dion et Bouton made their own sparking plugs and coils and even, for a time, their own batteries.

Batteries, and the difficulty of keeping them charged, were the pioneer motorists' *bêtes noirs*. On one or two makes, such as Mors and Packard, small dynamos were fitted to charge the batteries *en route*, but in general the difficulty of making small dynamos which would keep within a narrow voltage range at different engine speeds defeated designers until about 1910 when the growing popularity of electric lighting focussed effort on the problem. The great step in emancipating the motorist from the tyranny of his accumulator came with the introduction of magneto ignition.

The magneto was, indeed, no more than a simple permanent-magnet dynamo and the problem was to make it furnish sparks at the appropriate intervals without the intervention of battery and coil. The first solution was to use the low-voltage current from the magneto (which could not jump a gap under compression in a cylinder as a high-voltage current can) to strike an arc inside the combustion space by means of moveable contact pieces mechanically operated by some form of cam and tappet mechanism. This was 'low tension magneto ignition' which

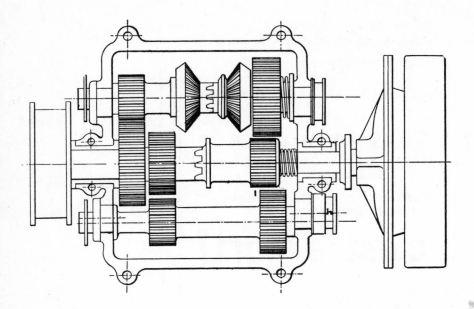

had been in use on some gas engines since about 1870. It had the great advantage of avoiding all difficulties with insulating high tension coils and circuits, and the disadvantage of needing fairly frequent adjustment of the delicate moving contacts in the cylinder heads which were subjected to great heat. This difficulty was overcome by Lanchester with typical ingenuity by a form of low-tension 'igniter', as he called it, which could be adjusted with a screw-driver while the engine was running, or removed and replaced in a few seconds without using any tools. This was in 1897, and was accompanied by Lanchester's own form of magneto which was made as part of the flywheel where the weight of the big magnets could be put to good use.

At about the same time Frederick Simms devised a form of low-tension magneto which was perfected by Robert Bosch and used on some of the Cannstatt-Daimler models in 1899. The Simms-Bosch low-tension magneto ignition was one of the talking points of Daimler's famous 'Mercedes' model in 1901, and thereafter many of the leading firms in the luxury-car class fitted low-tension magneto ignition. The next step was to combine the low tension magneto with a high tension coil

RENAULT GEARBOX, 1898

Renault's patent gearbox of 1898; the first to provide a direct drive— by coupling the two halves of the main centre shaft together by the jaw-clutch and leaving the lay-shafts out of mesh as shown. When required, one or another of the lay-shafts was swung sideways into mesh with the main-shaft. They were mounted in eccentric bushes to allow for this. The bevel gears meshed with a third bevel, not shown, to provide reverse.

(wound upon the same armature), and distributor, so as to do away with the complexity of the moving contact points inside the cylinders.

By late 1903 Robert Bosch and Co. had produced a satisfactory high-tension magneto, and within a few years similar magnetos were standard equipment on practically every make of motor car. As it took a good deal of effort to 'swing' a big engine fast enough, particularly in cold weather, to induce a spark from the magneto, luxury cars were fitted with both magneto and coil; the latter being used for starting and as a standby. During most of our period the Simms-Bosch magneto held pride of place in Europe and England, whilst Splitdorf and Eisemann shared the honours in America.

The lubricating arrangements of early car engines were haphazard in the extreme and generally worked a good deal better than they had any business to do. In essence most makers depended on 'splash lubrication', which merely meant that oil in the crankcase, which was very small by modern standards, was supposed to be kept at such a level that the connecting rods could just dip into it and churn it about so the bearings, cylinder walls, gudgeon-pins etc were well spattered. Transverse webs, or sheet metal troughs, were usually provided to keep the level below each big-end bearing more or less constant when the car was climbing or descending hills, and the big-ends themselves were often fitted with little oil scoops; although Sir Harry Ricardo demonstrated that these really served little purpose and that oil would reach the inside of the bearing just as well (or badly) whether the scoops were facing the direction of rotation, turned their backs upon it or were removed altogether.

The oil supply in the base chamber was supplemented by a tank-cum-drip-feed device on the dash board which fed oil through 'sight glasses' by gravity to the main engine bearings, timing-gears, etc. Overflow from these points was supposed to help keep the oil in the base up to the proper level, and could be supplemented by a hand-pump on the dashboard which fed a charge of fresh oil to crankcase or cylinder walls.

The oil in the dashboard tank was forced to the drip-feeds by exhaust pressure, by the circulation of the cooling water or, most often, by a little plunger pump in the tank driven by belt and pulley, or some mechanical linkage from the engine.

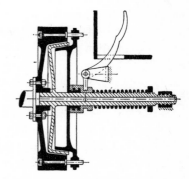

PANHARD-LEVASSOR CONE CLUTCH

The early Panhard-Levassor arrangement of cone clutch and clutch pedal; unless it was neglected or abused this clutch was very sweet in action.

This 'total loss' or 'drip and splash' system had some obvious hazards. The driver had to keep an eye on little drops of oil falling in little glass tubes, and adjust the needle valves above them if necessary. From the drip-feeds the supply was wholly dependent on gravity through a number of small-bore pipes which might become choked or broken from vibration, and there was really no way of telling whether the engine was getting sufficient oil except by adjusting the drips, or working the hand pump, until a nauseous cloud of oily smoke from the exhaust assured the motorist that his bearings were safe, whilst confirming the anti-motorist in his hatred of those 'filthy, stinking motors'.

To ensure adequate lubrication most engine designers made the crankshaft bearings very long by present day standards, but in order to reduce peripheral speeds the journals were small in diameter. This meant that crankshafts for multi-cylinder engines were very long and 'whippy', like so much mangled fence-wire by comparison with a modern crankshaft, and this aggravated the torsional vibration problem and hampered the search for increasing efficiency by raising rotational speeds.

Motor journals and catalogues of the period often refer to 'pressure lubrication' but this term, at first, only meant that the oil was forced to the drip-feeds by exhaust pressure (by a small-bore pipe from the exhaust manifold). In the modern sense 'pressure lubrication', by means of an oil pump in the base chamber forcing oil through a hollow crankshaft to the big-ends, gudgeon-pins and other vital parts, was one of Dr. Lanchester's innovations with the 4-and 6-cylinder models he designed in 1904. Similar lubrication by direct feed to the bearings under pressure had been done before on high speed steam engines, and one or two car manufacturers, notably Delaunay-Belleville, claim equal priority with Lanchester; with the important difference, however, that his system was run at a much higher pressure than theirs. Dr. Lanchester maintained that at least 35 - 40 1bs. per sq. in. was necessary to be sure of adequate lubrication under all conditions in engines capable of more than 2,000 r.p.m. This is the figure commonly accepted to-day.

Acceptance was slow in coming. Many extremely worthy motor cars, made on both sides of the Atlantic, still relied on 'splash' until the 1930's, though the drip feeds and exposed pipes had long since been abandoned in favour of much bigger base chambers and proper methods of ensuring

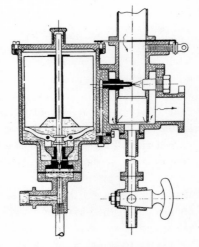

PEUGEOT CARBURETTOR,
1899

The spray from the horizontal jet impinged upon a conical plug which was supposed to help atomize the drops of fuel.

DE DION BOUTON 8, 1904

1-cylinder engine. Swept vol. 57.5 cu.ins.
8 h.p. at approx. 1,500 r.p.m. Constant
mesh expanding-clutch 3-speed gearbox
and final drive similar to the earlier rear-
engined models. Top speed about 34
m.p.h. France.

OLDSMOBILE 7, 1904

1-cylinder horizontal engine. Swept vol.
112 cu.ins. 7 h.p. at approx. 750 r.p.m.
2-speed and reverse epicyclic gearbox and
final drive by single chain to live axle. USA.

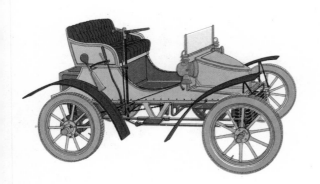

VAUXHALL, 1904

1-cylinder horizontal engine, 5 h.p. Swept
vol. 62.6 cu.ins. Epicyclic 2-speed gear.
Chain driven. Great Britain.

4.h.p. Single cylinder forward-mounted engine - the prototype front-engined Fiat which replaced the original rear-engined Voiturette of 1899. Italy.

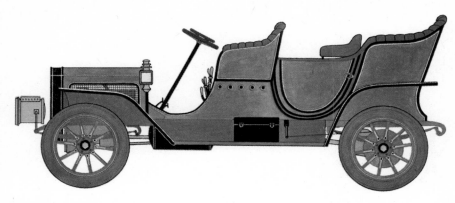

WHITE STEAM CAR, 1906

2-cylinder compound steam engine, with semi-flash boiler and paraffin burning furnace. Shaft-drive to live axle with emergency low gear for steep hills. USA.

ISOTTA-FRASCHINI, 1910

4-cylinder engine, approx. 30 h.p. Swept vol. 488 cu.ins. Luxury automobile in the same class as the Rolls-Royce and Lanchester. Italy.

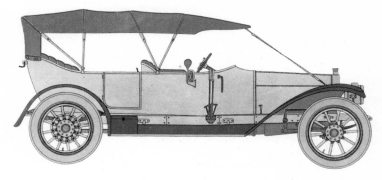

BUICK, MODEL C, 1905
2-cylinder horizontal engine, 22 h.p. 2-
speed and reverse epicyclic gearbox and final drive by single chain to live axle. USA.

MARCHAND LIMOUSINE, 1905
4-cylinder motor, 22 h.p. Swept vol. 331 cu.ins. Magneto ignition. Chain driven. Weight 3,080 1bs. Many similarities with Mercedes. Italy.

POPE-WAVERLEY, 1905
Electrically driven car with 60 volt D.C. motor. Accumulators provide range of approximately 30 miles without re-charging. USA.

RENAULT, 1906

4-cylinder side-valve engine, 30 h.p. at approx. 1,200 r.p.m. Cone clutch, 4-speed gearbox and, of course, shaft drive and live axle which Louis Renault used on all his cars including his first model of 1898. France.

OAKLAND, 1908

2-cylinder water-cooled engine, 20 h.p. Epicyclic gear box with 2 speeds. USA.

FIAT GRAND PRIX RACING CAR, F2, 1907

4-cylinder engine. 130 h.p. 7.2″ × 6.3″ bore and stroke. Swept vol. 995 cu.ins. Low tension magneto ignition. Final drive by side chains. Won 1907 G.P. Race at average speed of 70.5 m.p.h.

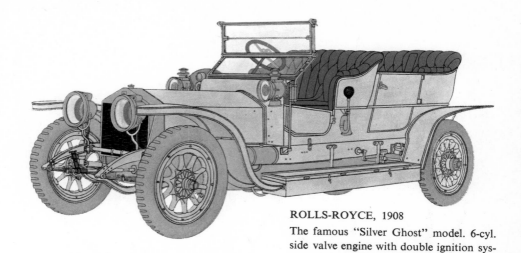

ROLLS-ROYCE, 1908

The famous "Silver Ghost" model. 6-cyl. side valve engine with double ignition system. Swept vol. 429 cu.ins. 48.3 h.p. 4-speed gearbox with direct drive on 3rd gear and "overdrive" 4th speed. In production, with slight variations only, 1906-1924. Great Britain.

LANCIA, TYPE 51, 1908

4-cylinder engine. Swept vol. 155.5 cu.ins. 15 h.p. at 1,800 r.p.m. Multi-disc clutch. 3 speeds. Top speed about 56 m.p.h. Italy.

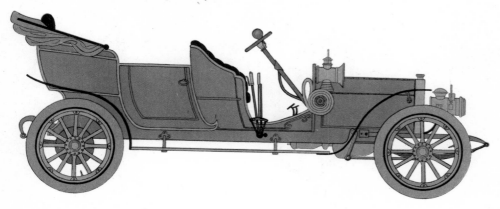

FORD MODEL T, 1909

4-cylinder side-valve engine with fly-wheel magneto and removable cylinder head. 20 h.p. Swept vol. 176.5 cu.ins. Pedal-controlled 2-speed epicyclic gear. In production 1908-1927. Not all the early Model T Fords were black. USA.

the correct oil-level. Lubrication under pressure was uncommon except on top-grade cars before the 1914 war, and only very few followed Lanchester in the use of high-pressure oiling.

Not a few cars were advertised as having 'pressure' or 'pump' lubrication although in reality the oil pump did no more than squirt jets of oil in the direction of the crank throws. On some cars arrangements were made automatically to augment the lubrication at full-throttle. On the Rolls-Royce 'Silver Ghost', for example, opening the throttle more than half way also opened a valve which allowed oil to be fed direct to the cylinder walls, whilst on the sleeve-valve Daimlers (which were splash-lubricated) the troughs into which the big-ends dipped were linked with the accelerator pedal, so that the wider the throttle opening the deeper the splash and the more offensive the exhaust smoke.

Articles and letters by the score in motor journals make it clear that after tyre and ignition troubles the pioneer motorist suffered much anxiety from overheating. In part the difficulty arose because most 'experts' assured the puzzled amateurs that overheating was a symptom of running with too *rich* a mixture, advised the admission of more air, and so aggravated the disease.

The early Benz and Panhard cars, though water cooled, had no radiators and the water in the tanks was merely allowed to boil away—though Benz did fit laughably inefficient annular condensers which condensed a minute fraction of the escaping steam and returned it to the tank. A quite extravagant weight of water had, in consequence, to be carried.

The first radiators on Panhard-Levassor cars were hung from the back of the chassis where they soon became choked with dust and mud and, where the necessary length of piping, and the inefficiency of the pump, driven by a friction disc from the rim of the flywheel, were sufficient to make leaks and air-locks almost inevitable. This layout was copied on the English Daimlers, but most other manufacturers realised that the front of the car was a better place for the radiator than the back. Until 1901, however, the radiator was generally hung below the chassis, rather than mounted above it, and it was not until Cannstatt-Daimler led the way that radiator and water tank were combined in one neat unit.

These early radiators consisted of one or more banks of large-bore

THORNYCROFT, 1903

1903 10 h.p. 2-cylinder Thornycroft, made by a firm famous for steam engines and heavy lorries. They made private cars from 1903 to 1913.

piping, with radiating fins of some kind attached, twisted to and fro in a rather untidy stack. As this was not a very efficient arrangement the water tank, almost invariably separate from the cooling coils, still had to hold an amount of water we should consider excessive. A 6 h.p. car might well be expected to cart a hundredweight of water about.

Many of the overheating troubles arose not from the cooling systems as such, but from poor design of the water ways in the cylinder heads and valve areas, giving rise to local heating, distortion, burnt valves and cracked cylinders. Although it is now fashionable to deride Carl Benz as a reactionary old fuddy-duddy it must be said that even his earliest car engines were admirably designed in this respect, and owe much of their reliability to the generous water ways round the valve areas.

CLEMENT-BAYARD, 1913

By 1905 Adolphe Clement had interests in so many firms (British Clement, Clement-Talbot, Clement-Garrads, Gladiator etc. etc.) that he agreed not to sell cars under his own name; but he started yet another business and the cars produced by it were called Bayards or Clement-Bayards.

Early water pumps were undeniably troublesome. Certainly, all those who copied Panhard-Levassor in slinging the pump below the chassis and relying upon a mud- and oil-splashed friction disc to drive it should have expected trouble; but even those pumps which were housed and driven in more civilised fashion appear to have leaked and failed in a great variety of perverse and ingenious ways. It might seem odd that the apparently simple task of making a reliable circulating pump should have defeated so many motor engineers, but as a neighbour of the writer has had five water pumps fail on his new Hillman Imp in 24,000 miles it is clear that the problem is still unsolved after some seventy years.

The clumsy tubular radiator soon gave way to a neater and more efficient arrangement of small-bore pipes in series, combined, generally, with small 'header' and bottom tanks in the modern fashion. Some makers preferred a cross-tube arrangement and the practice rapidly developed of making the radiator, handsomely encased and topped with brass, the distinctive feature of the car.

One of the talking points of the Mercedes of 1901 was the 'honeycomb' radiator which consisted, in effect, of a shallow vertical tank pierced by more than 5,000 small square-section air tubes (hexagonal tubes were later used by many firms), so that a thin film of water separated each tube from its neighbours. This expensive arrangement was extremely efficient and allowed a large engine to be cooled by a very small amount of water. Contrary to popular belief the 'honeycomb' was not an innovation on the first Mercedes model, but had already been proved on earlier Cannstatt-Daimler products on which it excited little attention. It was based on the marine condenser principle and the first description of it in the English technical press referred to it as the 'beehive cooler'. This bizarre title arose from some journalist's literal translation from the French *nid des abeilles*. As with so many Mercedes features the honeycomb radiator was widely copied on the more expensive cars, particularly in England.

It is impossible in this short work to trace other aspects of engine design, or to touch upon the fascinating developments in foundry techniques, machine shop practice, machine tool design, 'mass production' and the science of metallurgy which arose with the new industry. It is enough to say here that in the thirty years from Benz's first experimental

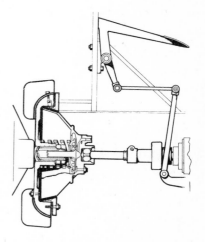

RENAULT CONE CLUTCH

The cone clutch of a 1908 2-cylinder Renault. The early Renault cars were admirably designed for ease of maintenance and the complete clutch assembly of this model could be dismantled in ten minutes.

car, specific output of the internal combustion engine rose from $\frac{1}{2}$ h.p. per litre to some 12-15 h.p. per litre for ordinary production models. Some racing car engines had already reached 30 h.p. per litre by 1914.

Chassis and suspension arrangements soon became stereotyped and generally speaking differed only in scale between the smallest and the largest types of conventional cars. The earliest cars had smaller wheels in front than those behind; this had been necessary with the center-pivoted axles of horse drawn vehicles to allow the wheels to 'lock over' for sharp curves. When it became apparent, about 1900, that unequal sized wheels were unnecessary with 'Ackermann' steering, the automobile stopped being a 'horseless carriage' and became recognizably a motor car. Except, of course, for those curious anomalies the American 'high-wheelers' or motorised buggies which remained popular in the farming districts of the middle west until as late as 1912.

The nineteenth century chassis designer could choose between the Panhard-Levassor type of timber frame, strengthened with flitch plates, or the tubular steel framing, inspired by the bicycle and favoured by most European and American makers of light cars. The wooden chassis never went completely out of favour, but after 1903 it was uncommon for any but light cars or cycle cars, in marked contrast to its role in the 1890's. Many of the tubular frames, by good makers, were admirably rigid, durable, and light. The brazed joints had to be carefully made and inspected, and chassis failures on cut-price machines brought the tubular chassis into disrepute.

One of the many myths about the Mercedes of 1901 is that it was the first car in the world to have a pressed steel chassis. Its immediate predecessor, the 24 h.p. 1899 'Phoenix' Daimler also had a steel girder frame, and one probably would not have to look far to find other, and earlier, examples. Many of the chassis which were described as 'pressed' steel were in reality composed of rolled channel section girders with rolled, or pressed, cross members rivetted to them. Even Henry Royce's first cars were assembled in this way, and their frail-looking bolted-on dumb-irons would not meet with much approval to-day.

As the advantages of making the side members, with dropped or in-curved sections, and integral with the dumb-irons or spring-horns, became manifest the technique of steel stamping on a large scale was

quickly developed. Though the leading makers continued to make their own chassis for some while, the specialist chassis maker soon came into his own. One of the most remarkable pieces of press-work was to be found on the Darracqs of 1903 onwards; the complete chassis, all but the rearmost cross member, was pressed from one piece. Because the engine position prevented the use of cross members in front, and because most engines and gear-boxes were mounted on sub-frames and could not therefore stiffen the frame, some firms used a combination stiffening-web-cum-engine-undershield to give front end rigidity. The Dutch Spyker carried this to a logical conclusion by extending the undershield, itself a light but rigid pressing, the full length of the chassis. This meant all the working parts were protected from dust and damp, and the absence of protuberances to create eddies and suck up the road surface earned for the cars the name of the 'Dustless Spyker'.

The road springs of the first motor cars were copied, not unnaturally, from the carriage springs of the time. That is to say they were laminated plate, or 'leaf' springs, of curved form assembled as half- three-quarter- or full-ellipses. The full-elliptic spring, used in the early days, did not

DAIMLER, 1905

1905, Daimler with the finned radiator which was the distinctive feature of the English Daimlers.

survive long (as it allowed too much side away at motor car speeds) except in America where those two unconventional masterpieces, the air-cooled Franklin and the Stanley steam car, were mounted on full-elliptics until very late.

The most usual arrangement after 1900 was to have the front axle suspended upon a pair of longitudinal half elliptic springs, with a rather wider choice of springs for the back axle. Three-quarter elliptics were popular for a long while, and up to about 1910 'platform suspension' was also widely used. This consisted of a pair of conventional longitudinal semi-elliptic springs, with the back axle mounted above or below them, shackled at their rear ends not directly to the chassis but to a third, inverted, semi-elliptic spring running across the back of the chassis to which it was clamped at its central point.

There were variations on the theme; some cars had a transverse spring for the front axle but few copied the Model T Ford with its transverse springing at both ends. Present day motor experts invariably write disparagingly of leaf springs and deride the cars which still have them as 'cart-sprung'. This overlooks the facts that the majority of horse-drawn carts had no springs at all, and that the merits or demerits of any particular suspension system depend much less on the choice of the elastic medium than in the mode of its application.

Helical springs, generally miscalled coil-springs, now so widely used, were occasionally seen on early cars. Some of the Cannstatt-Daimler models of the 1890's had helical springs between the rear under-frame and the carriage body. One American runabout, the Brush, was unique in having helical springs front and back, using them in tension not under compression and furthermore in attaching them to wooden axle beams.

Most pre-1914 cars had no rebound dampers, the designers reckoned that the natural self-damping action of the leaf springs was sufficient; considering the modest speeds of which most cars were capable they were undoubtedly right. Racing soon made the need for some additional damping apparent at higher speeds, and the first recorded use of dampers was on the 70 h.p. Mors which Gabriel drove in the Paris-Madrid race of 1903. Commandant Krebs, of Panhard-Levassor, had, however, patented an admirable face-cam damper some years earlier, and the Columbia Carriage and Cycle Company were also early in the field with

PEUGEOT, 1905

A small Peugeot of 1905: this family firm is one of the few independent companies left — still in the motor business after 75 years.

the 'Hartford' shock absorber which became particularly well known in the 1920's.

With large diameter wheels, small unsprung weight and relatively low speeds, independent suspension was not as necessary before 1914 as it is for the very different conditions which apply to-day. Nevertheless, some few makes had independent front wheel suspension at a very early period. The Stephens of 1898 and the Decauville of 1899 are examples which come to mind, but the best known example, a few years later, is the Sizaire-Naudin which used a combination of sliding pillar and transverse leaf spring almost identical with the arrangement now to be found on the highly successful Dutch Daf.

As early as 1900 Dr. Lanchester demonstrated the requirements for good road-holding, comfortable riding and the best possible tyre life. These were that the chassis should be absolutely rigid and torsionally stiff, and the suspension 'soft, with the spring rates equal to the normal adult walking pace' (about 80-90 vibrations a minute), and that the wheels must be constrained to rise and fall in a truly vertical path in relation to the longitudinal line of the car and not in the arc of a circle as with the normal methods of the time. These conditions were fulfilled in the Lanchester cars by chassis girders of aluminium and steel eighteen inches in depth, combined with very long cantilever springs and parallel-motion radius and torque links.

The easy riding of the Lanchester was unequalled until comparatively recently, and by about 1909 many other manufacturers had started to copy the cantilever springing; few, however, used it both front and back, as Lanchester did, and fewer still copied the parallel motion linkwork which, in a different form, is now to be seen in the 'wishbone' linkage of many modern suspension systems.

Few early designers appreciated the dictum that the springs should be as supple as possible and the chassis as rigid as it could be made. Many manufacturers, perhaps unwittingly, relied on the flexing of the chassis to mitigate the inadequacy of their springs but on the whole it must be admitted that the majority of pre-1914 motor cars were very much better sprung than the horse drawn carriages they replaced.

They were also infinitely better braked. This was not difficult as many horsed vehicles were virtually brakeless and dependent upon the horse's

NAPIER SIXTY, 1907
A 6-cylinder Napier Sixty of 1907. The 6-cylinder Napiers were always marred by their clumsy-looking forward-thrust radiators which made them look nose-heavy.

ability to 'hold back' for an emergency stop, and relied on the barbaric, road-destroying, skid-pan for descending steep hills. The road accident rate, in consequence, was proportionately greater seventy years ago than it is now.

Almost from the start most cars had two independent braking systems (some had three), but it must be remembered that many cars had unthrottled, constant speed, engines and consequently the value of engine braking was not realised and many cars were so arranged that application of the brakes automatically declutched the engine. This practice continued in France even after the modern concept of driving on the throttle pedal had become established. A number of accidents did, in consequence, occur on long steep hills from brake failure as the lining materials, adequate enough for ordinary purposes, were easily charred and made useless if applied too long.

Most brakes before 1900 were of the contracting band variety, though some cars had one pair of brakes acting directly upon the rear tyres. Though good in theory these were bad in practice as in wet weather they did not grip and in dry weather, at motor car speeds, they might work too well and rip the tyres from the rims. They were usually only fitted on solid tyred cars and were, in consequence, almost extinct before the end of the nineteenth century.

A peculiarity of the band brakes of the early days was that so many makers fell into the error of copying Panhard-Levassor too slavishly and using a single-acting band mechanism which tended to have a self-wrapping action in the forward direction but which, in reverse, unwrapped and consequently lost nine tenths of the efficiency. Therefore if the engine failed, or a driving chain broke, or (most common hazard) the driver missed a gear change whilst climbing, the car could run back and get out of control. To deal with this many cars were fitted with a sprag, or stout pointed iron bar, hinged to the underside of the chassis and normally held clear of the ground by a cord or wire. On approaching a hill the driver was supposed to release the cord so that the sprag trailed on the ground at an angle of about 45 degrees, so as to dig into the surface and hold the vehicle should it start to run back. Quite soon the folly of these one-way-only brakes was realised and double-action mechanism was used to actuate the bands; but many motorists con-

SPYKER, 1905

1905 4-cylinder Spyker. This Dutch firm produced several interesting designs including the first 6-cylinder car in 1903. This model has an 18 h.p. engine (90 × 100 mm) with a ball-bearing crankshaft

tinued to have sprags fitted as they were a great convenience when obliged to stop and re-start on a steep gradient.

Brake linings were, at first, generally of leather though woven camel hair and similar fabrics were occasionally used. These materials were quite effective but were very short lived and easily burnt out. Woven asbestos materials did not come into use until 1905 and were not common for some years. Many cars during the last half of our period had metal-to-metal brakes—brass facings, for instance, acting in or upon cast iron drums — which worked well, were not so quickly made ineffective by heat as leather but were apt to become very noisy when hot.

Soon after the turn of the century most good quality cars had internal expanding drum brakes, almost invariably hand-operated, on the rear wheels, but the pedal brake, acting upon some part of the transmission shafting, was still very often of the contracting band, or external shoe variety. Contracting brakes on the wheel drums were still, however, to be found on light cars, and many American makes, until relatively late.

Some fast and heavy cars, such as Mercedes, Delaunay-Belleville and Gobron-Brillié, had two independent foot-brake systems operating on different parts of the transmission and each with its own pedal. This was done not so much to provide spectacular stopping power (for the braking effort was still confined to the rear wheels only) but to prevent overheating the brakes by using them alternately. Early Mercedes models had a water drip arrangement to cool the transmission brakes, but Hispano-Suiza went one better with hollow aluminium brake shoes connected to the cooling system.

It became obvious quite soon that the transmission footbrake imposed severe strains upon the final drive gears, the chains, or the universal joints of shaft driven vehicles. As experience grew, many motorists therefore fell into the habit of 'driving on the hand brakes' and keeping the footbrake in reserve for emergencies. After about 1910 many makers' instruction books advocated this practice, but the logical step of making the footbrake operate on or in the rear wheel drums was not immediately taken. American and German manufacturers led the way in this so obvious, and so sensible, development but most French and English cars were still fitted with pedal operated transmission brakes into the nineteen twenties.

DE DION VIS-À-VIS

One of the popular little rear-engined De Dion Bouton voiturettes showing the vis-à-vis seating arrangement. The detachable canopy did not really afford much protection and soon went out of fashion.

Even the best of these 2-wheel braking systems were feeble by modern standards, but they were perfectly adequate for the speeds and traffic densities of the time. Brakes on all four wheels were often advocated, and occasionally fitted, before 1914. There were also experiments with 'diagonal braking' — footbrake working, say, on offside front wheel and nearside rear, whilst the handbrake took effect on the other two — which seems to have been somewhat less lethal than one would suppose. Rather curiously, the two principal Scottish manufacturers, Arrol-Johnston and Argyll, were the leading practitioners of four-wheel braking before 1914, but in general it must be regarded as a post war development.

Having briefly discussed the machinery which propelled the early petrol car when all was well, and the brakes which brought it to a halt when providence was kind, we must consider the transmission system which, said the steam car advocates, was so complicated that the internal combustion vehicle could not possibly survive.

Whether or not Levassor actually said of his change speed gearing that '*it was brutal but it worked*', the brutality was glaringly apparent and it is distinctly odd that the Levassor system, modified and improved but basically unaltered, continued to plague the average unskilled motorist for some seventy years, as many less brutal arrangements were perfected at an early date.

ARROL-JOHNSTON, 1902

The Arrol-Johnston motor dogcart of 1902. Made in Scotland this car had a most interesting 2-cylinder opposed piston engine. Despite its primitive appearance it was a very sound design well suited to heavy work over bad roads.

Apart altogether from the difficulties imposed by the inflexibility of the early engines, with their atmospheric inlet valves and primitive carburettors, the conventional system had a built-in stumbling block for the mechanically unskilled in that precise co-ordination of hand and foot, and a keen ear for engine speeds, were required in order to change gear without the 'prolonged side-grubbing of teeth', or 'the jarring and clashing of changing speeds' which figure so prominently in the motor journals of the day. When engines became more flexible, and instantly responsive to a foot- or hand-throttle, the business became easier, but only a fraction of the world's drivers acquired the sensitivity and dexterity needed to practise the technique of 'double de-clutching' so as to be sure of making a smooth, silent gear change at all times. Even when synchromesh mechanism made its appearance in the late nineteen-twenties the co-ordination of clutch pedal and gear lever was still beyond the grasp of many.

Consequently the shriek of tortured cog-wheels was regarded as inevitable, and most drivers avoided changing gear as much as possible. Apart from the racing driver, the use of the gearbox as an aid to acceleration was not practised and the car which could go anywhere and climb anything in top gear was the one the average buyer wanted. This was a good thing in encouraging the search for greater flexibility and low speed torque, but these characteristics were often provided at the expense of reasonable performance at the top end of the scale.

This dread of the gear-changing process was, and still is, particularly evident among American motorists, which is why the four-speed gearbox, always *de rigeur* on good quality European cars, was less common in America, and also explains the popularity of the epicyclic or 'planetary' gear in the United States.

The belt and pulley change speed system of the Benz and its imitators had needed no co-ordination of hand and foot, and would have been almost fool-proof if the perverse Carl Benz had not arranged all the controls so inconveniently. It had also been almost noiseless and the elasticity of the belts had helped damp out the jerky impulses of the slow-running single-cylinder engine. Alas, this simple mechanism took up a lot of room and did not take kindly to transmitting the higher power that was expected as time went on. Final drive by rubber and canvas

PANHARD LEVASSOR
An under-the-bonnet view of a 2-cylinder 6 h.p. Panhard-Levassor of 1898/99. The radiator is at the back of the chassis.

V-belting was used on tricars and cycle cars, but the belt and pulley primary drive of the original Benz type was obsolescent by 1900 and extinct by 1903.

One of Louis Renault's important contributions to the motor car was his patent gearbox of 1898, which gave a 'direct drive', with no gear wheels transmitting power, on the high gear. This was an improvement on the Panhard type which transmitted each speed indirectly through a pair of gear wheels, thus entailing noise and frictional losses. Renault's gearbox also had the oddity that the toothed wheels for the indirect speeds were not slid longitudinally into mesh, but met tooth-face to tooth-face. This somewhat alarming arrangement was not continued beyond 1905 and was not copied by others, but by about 1903 the majority of manufacturers had adopted different forms of 'direct drive' gearbox. Generally the direct drive was arranged for the highest gear, but there were exceptions; among the best known were the Rolls-Royce light Twenties, Thirties and early Silver Ghosts on all of which the third gear was direct, and the fourth, in consequence, became a geared-up overdrive for use on down gradients or long stretches of straight road which could be taken at speed.

As time went on gear wheels became smaller and their tooth formation more accurately calculated; also the gear shafts became shorter and more rigid, all of which helped make the conventional gearbox quieter and easier to handle. One fundamental improvement was the 'selective' or 'gate' gear change developed by Cannstatt-Daimler during the 'nineties and publicised on the appearance of the first Mercedes model in 1901. The Panhard-Levassor system, so widely copied, had been 'progressive'; that is, the gear lever had moved in the arc of a circle, over a notched quadrant, or sector, so that moving the lever to the neutral position from the top gear notch had entailed going through all the intermediate speeds. The Mercedes selective gear change was widely copied in England and America (where it seems first to have been used by Packard in 1902), but a number of French cars were still made with 'quadrant change' up to 1914. One suspects that French reluctance to pay royalties to a German firm had something to do with this.

Many different sorts of clutch mechanism were evolved between 1895 and 1914, and most manufacturers made their own; though there were

F.N., 1910
1910, 4-cylinder 12 h.p. F.N. One of the fine cars made in Belgium.

a few proprietary clutches such as the Hele-Shaw and the Weston. There were single plate and multi plate clutches, dry clutches and oil-immersed ones, expanding clutches, contracting clutches and many more. One type, however, predominated during the whole period; this was the cone clutch with friction facings almost always of leather.

Writers of motor history. some of whom, one suspects, have never actually driven any of the machines they pontificate about, have implied that the cone clutch was a crude affair, and inherently so fierce in action that no early car could be started from rest without leaping like a kangaroo. This is not so. The cone clutch certainly tends to become fierce with wear or misuse, but if properly designed (as the majority were), and kept in order, it is as sweet as one could wish. Which is why it had so long a life and was used by so many firms whose names became synonymous with refinement, such as Rolls-Royce in England, Chadwick in America, Minerva in Belgium and Delaunay-Belleville in France. Even Daimler in Germany, who had been faithful to the Mercedes 'scroll' or coil spring clutch for so long, changed to the conical variety in 1914.

Whatever form the clutch took it was generally recessed into, or formed part of, the flywheel, and the almost universal practice at first was to have the gearbox separated from the engine and connected to the clutch by a 'jack shaft', with some kind of flexible joint in it to allow for relative movements between engine and gearbox set up by chassis flexure. Integral construction of engine, clutch housing and gearbox was practised quite early, and leaders in this innovation were Motobloc in France and Lanchester in England. The lead was followed in America and gained ground there very quickly when Henry Ford adopted this style of construction for his Model T, but it was less common on this side of the Atlantic, despite its European origin.

Almost as many alternatives to the conventional gearbox as there were to the cone clutch were offered in the first years of the century. The most successful commercially (because of their relatively large output) was the De Dion Bouton arrangement in which the gears were always in mesh, and those on the output shaft were clutched to it as required by ingenious expanding clutches contained in small drums attached to the gear wheels. The lever on the steering column, in con-

LANCHESTER, 1904

1904 12 h.p. Lanchester with the vibrationless double-crank engine shown on pages 34 and 35. The Lanchester cars had worm-gear final drive, cantilever suspension and pre-selector 3-speed epicyclic gears.

junction with a form of pre-selector on the later 3-speed models, which controlled the clutches, gave the driver an easy means of starting smoothly and changing gear without the usual correlation of hand and foot.

Other easy-to-drive systems, such as the Barber hydraulically controlled progressively variable gearbox, the Lentz hydraulic transmission, the Mercedes-Mixte petrol electric, the Owen Magnetic, and very many more did not survive long. This was partly because they were ahead of their time, partly because of complication and cost but largely because the conventional system was too well established. Apart, therefore, from the De Dion Bouton system (which the firm finally gave up in 1908) the only real challenger to the sliding pinion gearbox was the epicyclic or 'planetary' gear. This also, in effect, had a separate clutch for each speed, generally in the form of a contracting brake acting upon the drum containing the epicyclic gear train in question. In consequence the epicyclic gearbox could be made easy to operate as one lever (with, perhaps, a separate control or pedal to select reverse) could select the gear required and with the same movement tighten the brake which brought that particular gear into play.

The ordinary simple type of epicyclic gear system gave a low speed and reverse and a direct-drive high gear. The provision of additional gear trains increased the cost and complication disproportionately and consequently the easy control of the planetary gear was bought at the cost of performance. The average American runabout of the first years of this century, for example, could bowl along on a level road at 25 m.p.h. or a little more, but once reduced to 'low' on a hill it was also reduced to a walking pace until level ground was reached again.

In 1898 Dr. Frederick Lanchester patented a system of compound epicyclic gears which enabled him to provide his cars with three forward speeds; control being by a pre-selector system of the utmost simplicity of operation. This 'compounding' was not copied by others for many years, but now forms the basis of most modern automatic gearboxes. For his Model T, Henry Ford devised an uniquely simple pedal control for the 2-speed planetary gearbox, and much of the well deserved popularity of the Tin Lizzie stemmed from the ease with which a novice could learn to drive it.

'UNIC' TAXI, 1908

Made by the firm of Georges Richard the 'Unic' taxi cabs, such as this 1908 model, were designed to meet London's strict Police specifications. With very little alteration the type remained in production for twenty years, and many individual cabs saw twenty five years continuous service.

Controversy raged furiously over the rival merits of chain or shaft drive. The former fell into two categories; the single chain and differential live axle of the American runabout or gas-buggy type of light car (found also on a few European models), or the differential countershaft, side chains and 'dead' axle of the Panhard-Levassor and some hundreds of others.

The combination of longitudinal propellor shaft and gear-driven live axle was used on the experimental Lanchester in 1896 and by Maxim in America in 1898, but both these examples had unsprung rear axles; Louis Renault made the innovation of putting universal joints in the drive shaft so that the axle might rise and fall on springs in the usual way.

For the first few years of the century the shaft and live axle combination was thought proper only for very small light vehicles, and although Renault, Itala, Napier, Lanchester and others soon showed that the shaft transmission was equally successful on powerful cars, the great majority of the larger machines retained their chain transmission for some years. The obvious disadvantages of noise, and the rapid wear of chains and sprockets exposed to mud and dust (few were enclosed), was supposed to be offset by less unsprung weight, less tyre wear and less risk of axle failure. By the end of our period chain drive was almost extinct on all but a few racing cars.

Nearly all the shaft driven cars had straight-toothed bevel gearing for the final drive. This tended to be noisy unless very carefully hand finished and fitted. Parallel-toothed worm gearing, though silent, was 'viewed with suspicion by most engineers of the time and Lanchester's unique form of 'hour-glass', or enveloping, worm gear, which he patented and used on his cars, was also derided in the technical press. As its durability and efficiency were amply demonstrated in the course of time many leading manufacturers, Daimler for instance, began using the Lanchester gear. It did not, however, have much following in the United States but some of the leading makers there began to use spiral bevel gearing, of the modern form, before 1914: this allowed the propellor shaft line to be lowered and was as quiet as worm gearing but less expensive to make.

There has always been an element in public and official opinion, particularly in England, which is opposed to the racing and sporting aspects of motoring, and which blames all road accidents, in the teeth of the evidence, on 'the insensate passion for speed'. Unfortunately a disproportionate weight is attached to the holders of these views, who bedevil every attempt to deal rationally with traffic and road accidents by dragging in emotive words like 'slaughter', 'maniac', 'lethal weapons', 'speed-crazed' and so forth. Indeed, one recent speaker, who should have known better, who appeared in a television discussion of road accidents proclaimed in passionate tones that the root of the trouble lay in the motorists' 'urge to kill'.

Nobody could defend the heedless motorist, generally inexperienced, who drives faster than his skill or the prevailing conditions warrant; nor is the rude, impatient fellow who thrusts and bullies his way through defensible. Also, the practitioners and devotees of motor sport, in all its branches, are apt to become single minded and boring, as enthusiasts so often do, and to despise those who do not choose always to drive at the very limit of safety.

Granted these premises it still cannot be denied that it is largely because of racing that an old fuddy-duddy like the writer is able to drive

JEANTAUD, 1899
Jeantaud electric car in which the Count de Chasseloup-Laubat set a record of 43.69 m.p.h. in January 1899. This was the first of the long series of officially recorded World's Land Speed Records.

about in comfort and safety at 60-70 m.p.h. in a little cheap motor car propelled by a tiny engine which would not have been thought big enough for anything but a motor tricycle seventy years ago. He can do so, moreover, in reasonable certainty that the tyres will not fail after 1,000 miles — indeed after 50,000 they will still be safe — that the machinery will not fall into the road and that should some absent minded old man or impetuous child step into his path he will be able to stop in time to avoid another fatality.

There is little doubt that it was the rapid development of well-organized racing in France which gave the French motor industry its early ascendancy. Equally, the fact that racing under the auspices of the A.C.F. was for many years conducted upon ordinary public highways greatly helped the development of the motor car during its formative years.

It is true that the 'racing car' and the 'touring car' became different branches of the same family as time went on, but the family connection remained intact. The freakish machines designed for that rather boring pastime, breaking the world's land speed record, and the cars built specially for relatively short track events in the early American style had much less influence than the true road racing car upon the improvement of the bread-and-butter automobiles sold to the public.

JEANTAUD, 1899

Another Jeantaud contender for the record; the Count de Chasseloup-Laubat reached 57.6 m.p.h. in this electric car, in April 1899, but was easily beaten by Jenatzy's 65.7 m.p.h.

This is no place for a blow-by-blow account of the most important races, hill-climbs, and long-distance trials of the time. Many thousands of words have been written upon these topics, and the reader who yearns to know the bore and stroke of the Landry et Beyroux in which the Marquis de Montaignac had a fatal accident during the *Course de Perigueux* in 1898, or the time of Stricker's fastest lap in his *Porthos* in the 1908 Grand Prix, will find ample reference material to guide him. We are here concerned to trace the ways in which, very broadly, the racing car developed and influenced, or was influenced by, the touring vehicle.

In the first motor races, both in France and elsewhere, no particular attempts at classification were made and machines of vastly different styles and potentialities were matched against one another. As we have seen, in the Paris-Bordeaux-Paris Race of 1895, Emile Levassor, though undeniably the 'winner', was not awarded the first prize as that was reserved for a car with seats for four: the race included 2- and 4-seater petrol cars, a Hilderbrandt and Wolfmuller motor bicycle, Amédée Bollée's 15 years old 10-seater steam 'bus and Jeantaud's 6-seat battery electric car—all competing on equal terms. In the following year some attempt at segregation was made. Class A was for cars, subdivided into those seating up to four persons and those with more than four seats, and Class B for motor cycles (a term which included tricycles and quadricycles) weighing less than 150 Kg., subdivided into those with and those without pedals. The big event of 1896, the Paris-Marseilles-Paris Race, for which eliminating trials had to be held because of the large number of entries in the cycle class, therefore included 'conventional' cars, two 15 h.p. De Dion Bouton steam 'brakes', and at the other end of the scale two $\frac{3}{4}$ h.p. De Dion petrol tricycles and four of Léon Bollée's tandem tricars. Though all raced over the same course (starting at one minute intervals) the different classes were timed separately.

The winner's speed in this event (Mayarde on 6 h.p. Panhard-Lavassor) was only half-a-mile an hour faster, at 15.7 m.p.h., than Lavassor's speed in the 1895 event, but the conditions were infinitely worse. Torrential storms of rain, hail and wind played havoc with ignition burners, belts and chains whilst the drivers had to cope with such uncanonical hazards as colliding by night (all having been delayed) with fallen trees,

JENATZY, 1899
Jenatzy's streamlined electric car, *La Jamais Contente*, — the first road vehicle to exceed 60 m.p.h. in April 1899.

unlighted coal carts and straying cows. The most significant result, not fully appreciated at the time, was that Viet's $^3/_4$ h.p. tricycle was only 0.6 m.p.h. slower on average than the most powerful petrol car in the race — the 4-cylinder 8 h.p. Panhard driven by Merkel.

Further segregation into classes took place during the next years but no very logical, orderly or uniform arrangements were agreed until after the end of the century. The Paris-Amsterdam-Paris Race of 1898 was not only the first 'classic' event to cross the French border but the first to be divided into 'tourist' and 'racing' classes. The former, obviously, had a less arduous task and took part, in effect, in a long distance demonstration run. The winner's speed now rose to 26.9 m.p.h.

By this time the pattern of the European racing calendar was well established, and the national motor clubs of France, Belgium and Germany, as well as a number of local clubs, ran sporting events of one kind and another, such as hill-climbs, reliability runs, speed contests over short distances and so forth. The culmination of each sporting year, however, was the big Town-to-Town race which, following the success of Paris-Amsterdam, generally spread over two or more countries and called for prodigious powers of organisation.

These Town-To-Town races were a purely European and primarily French phenomenon. It was so clearly unthinkable that Authority in England, wedded to the 12 m.p.h. limit of the 1896 Act and dominated by a rabidly anti-motorist lay magistracy, would permit racing on public highways that the English Club confined their efforts to promoting demonstrations and gymkhanas on private ground.

In America, two Town-to-Town races were organised: they were not unduly hampered by Authority but died of sheer inanition. These events were the the 'Times-Herald' contest over 54 miles in November 1895, and the New York 'Cosmopolitan' race over sixty miles on May 30th 1896. In the first event, two cars finished, after much manual help, and in the second only the Duryea managed the distance, trifling though it was by comparison with Paris-Bordeaux-Paris of the year before, at an average speed of less than 8 m.p.h. In his *Record of Motor Racing, 1894-1908* Gerald Rose justly observes that this: ' . . . was a complete fiasco, and thereby the self-propelled vehicle earned for itself a reputation which for a time severely damaged its future' .

SERPOLLET, 1902
Léon Serpollet, with this steam car, raised the record to 75.06 m.p.h. in April 1902.

For some while, therefore, American competition was confined to endurance contests and occasional short speed events on race tracks. The latter did not provide anything like so severe a test of machine and driver as the classic French races, but the long distance trials certainly tested the endurance of the human beings as well as the machines they drove, hauled or shoved through the quagmires. As late as 1903 the record time for the east to west coast journey stood at sixty one days (Packard, Model F.)

It is clear from contemporary records and journals that the American public, including most of the growing band of motor manufacturers, knew nothing of the distance by which they had been outstripped by the supposedly backward and decadent French. James Gordon Bennett, the newspaper magnate, did realise the gravity of the situation and determined to give his countrymen an incentive to catch up. He did so by offering the Automobile Club de France a valuable international trophy to be competed for not by individual firms or drivers, but by the representative clubs of different countries. The clubs were to hold eliminating contests to decide their representatives, and every part of every car so

MORS, 1902

The record was again raised in November 1902 to 77.13 m.p.h. with the 60 h.p. Mors—4-cylinders, 140 × 150 mm.

GOBRON-BRILLIÉ, 1903

The unconventional Gobron-Brillié, with a 4-cylinder, 8-piston (opposed pistons) engine of 100 h.p. (140 mm bore × 220 mm combined stroke) raised the land speed record to 84.73 m.p.h. in November 1903.

selected was to be made in the country of origin so that victory would be a source of national pride, as well as an advertisement for the manufacturer concerned.

After an orgy of bickering, squabbling, malice and all uncharitableness of the sort seemingly inseparable from the world of sport, the affair was settled and the first Gordon Bennett Race was held on the 14th of June, 1900, over the 353 miles from Paris to Lyons. It had not been taken very seriously, but the French, determined to uphold their superiority, had entered the maximum permitted number of three cars — all Panhard-Levassors. Germany did not bother, and the British motor enthusiasts were preoccupied with the Automobile Club's 1,000 Miles trial, so the only other competitors were a Bolide from Belgium and a Winton from America. This single-cylinder tiller-steered machine looked very primitive by comparison with the 24 h.p. 4-cylinder Panhards and dropped out of the race very soon. Despite incessant tyre troubles, and a back axle bent in crossing one of the *canniveaux* which traversed French highways at intervals, Charron's winning Panhard averaged 38.6 m.p.h. which clearly gave the Americans food for thought.

Speeds in the earliest motor races were so low that the onlookers, who were not many, were in little danger. As speeds rose so did the numbers of those who turned out to watch and the A.C.F. had increasing difficulty in getting permission to hold races. Speeds were supposed to be very strictly controlled in towns and villages (which posed problems for the marshals and timekeepers), and police, soldiery or race officials were supposed to keep the crowds out of danger. The controls and other safety measures were often inefficient or evaded, and although the major events were usually well organised, lesser affairs, arranged by the smaller clubs, gave ammunition to those who complained, often with very good reason, of the danger, noise, dust and general inconvenience of motor racing.

The Town-to-Town races, therefore, were doomed and the end came in 1903 when the authorities, horrified by the accidents and chaos, halted the Paris to Madrid Race at Bordeaux, ordered all the racing cars to be returned by rail to their respective bases and would not even allow them to be driven to the station — they had to be pushed or towed by horses.

FORD '999', 1903

Henry Ford's sprint car, '999', which had neither gearbox nor differential, was driven at 91.37 m.p.h. in January 1903 but was not officially timed for the record according to A.C.F. rules.

MERCEDES, 1904

This 90 h.p. (4-cylinder 165 × 140 mm) Mercedes took the land speed record at 92.3 m.p.h. in January 1904.

Many thousands of words have been written about the Paris-Madrid Race, and the inevitable journalistic title of '*The Race of Death*' has clung to it. Curiously enough, no writer, of the time or since, has been able to determine exactly how many people were killed, and it is likely that the business was by no means so bloody as popular imagination makes it. Almost certainly the fatalities were fewer than fifteen.

Two facts stand out: in view of the enormous crowds the police and soldiery detailed to guard the route were so pitifully few that disaster was inevitable, and the speed made by Gabriel, driving a 10-litre 4-cylinder Mors (rated at 70 h.p.), would still be remarkable today. Despite all the hazards, all the racing and touring cars which had been sent away before him (his starting number was 168), the blinding dust clouds and the inevitable tyre failures he covered the 342 miles racing distance at an *average* speed of 65.3 m.p.h. At every suitable opportunity (and at many which one might think unsuitable) he must have travelled at 80-90 m.p.h. This performance not only says all that needs to be said of M. Gabriel's skill and courage, but of the great strides the infant motor industry had made since 1895.

Improvements in chassis design, with longer wheelbases and lower centres of gravity, contributed greatly to the improved performance; and the inadequacy of the Panhard type of tiller steering had been demonstrated as early as 1897 when Emile Levassor himself was thrown from his car when the steering was jerked out of control during the Paris-Marseilles Race (he died of his injuries some ten months later). Though tube ignition was dead and automatic inlet valves moribund by 1903 the specific efficiency of engines had not been very greatly improved and impressive performances like Gabriel's were achieved by sheer brute force. In other words the calls for greater speed were answered by providing ever larger and larger engines.

The Town-to-Town races perished and were replaced by circuit racing which, in modern form, is still with us. It was, indeed, already practised before 1903 and although it lacked the sheer glamour of Town-to-Town racing the conditions could be made even more severe, by the choice of a suitable network of hilly, twisting country roads, and the total distance, of course, could be easily suited to different classes of event. At the same time as securing greater safety, by closing the circuit

GOBRON-BRILLIÉ, 1904
One hundred miles an hour was first officially 'broken' in July 1904 when Rigolly drove the opposed-piston Gobron-Brillié at 103.56 m.p.h.

of chosen roads on practise and race days, (they were generally in remote country districts) stands could be provided at strategic points, those without places in the stands could chose good vantage points and all the spectators could keep track of the progress of the race.

The pattern was followed in other lands. The first race for the Vanderbilt Cup in America, in October 1904, was held over an irregular triangular course of about 30 miles on Long Island, the total racing distance being 284.4 miles. This race, and its successors and imitators, gave the American manufacturers ample opportunity, which was eagerly seized upon, to catch up on European progress without the expense of sending cars and teams across the Atlantic.

The first two places in the first Vanderbilt Race were taken by Panhard-Levassor and Clément-Bayard respectively, and this pattern was repeated; it was not until 1908 (following disastrous casualties in 1906 there was no race in 1907) that an American motor car, a 90 h.p. 4-cylinder Locomobile, won the premier American event. Though absolute victory eluded the native designers during these years the margins were very narrow, and some of the American racing cars of this early period were of considerable technical interest. Some, indeed, such as the 8-cylinder Maxwell, the engine of which was so long that the driver sat behind the back axle, its even more bizarre sister the horizontally-opposed 12-cylinder car which had no flywheel, and the front-wheel-drive, transverse engined Christie bordered upon the freakish and generally did not succeed in getting through the eliminating contests; nevertheless they contained many ingenious features. The most successful contenders, on the other hand, including the Locomobile, were of conventional European pattern. The Packards, for instance, were Mors in all but name and the highly successful Thomas was based upon Berliet designs, the firm having obtained the services of Le Blon and Caillois and had pattern engines and other parts sent out from France.

As early as 1900 the amateur racing drivers (for the professional was scarcely known), and the national clubs, began to look askance at the monstrously powerful racing cars specially developed by manufacturers. Though they were very small beer compared with the giants of a few years later, owner drivers felt that the manufacturers' entries gave those who drove them an unfair advantage. Similarly the organising bod-

MERCEDES, 1904
The land speed record was raised to 97.26 m.p.h. by this 90 h.p. Mercedes in April 1904.

ies felt that the real encouragement of motoring as a serious mode of travel would be hindered rather than helped if monsters were encouraged to breed.

The Automobile Club de France classification in 1900-01, generally copied throughout Europe, was as follows:

Class A Cars having two places only, side by side, weighing more than 650 kg.

Class B Light cars: between 400-650 kg.

Class C Voiturettes; between 250-400 kg.

Class D Other vehicles, tricycles, tricars etc. weighing less than 250 kg.

Though these divisions were so generally satisfactory that they lasted, with one alteration, for six years the Commission Sportif became so alarmed at the shape the racing car was assuming that they added an upper weight limit of 1,000 kg. in 1902. As cars were brought to the weigh-in stripped of every possible accessory (even the seat cushions being removed on occassion) an extra 7 kg. was allowed for magneto ignition: the reason for this was that a magneto could not be readily removed but the accumulator for coil-ignition could be taken off and the car driven on to the weighbridge by means of a little pocket-lamp battery.

If the organising bodies hoped to curb the race of giants by this limit they were the more deceived, for all that happened was that designers exercised their ingenuity in cramming the largest possible engines, of the least possible weight, into chassis pared to the utmost edge of the safety limit — and beyond.

The modern approach towards increasing efficiency by raising the compression, by attention to manifold and combustion chamber shapes and above all by increasing rotational speeds was understood in theory but could not be put into practise because of various constructional and metallurgical shortcomings. Therefore, the 1,000 kg. limit did not directly improve specific efficiency, but a great deal was learnt about weight saving which was of benefit to the ordinary motorist in course of time.

It is often thought that concern to reduce weight is a fairly modern notion, and that the cars of the past were invariable heavy and ponderous. That this is not so is amply demonstrated by such a splendid folly, for example, as the famous 'Seventy Panhard' of 1902, in which a 13½

DARRACQ, 1904

Rigolly's record only stood for three months. Baras raised the figure to 104.5 m.p.h in this 100 h.p. (4-cyl. 160 × 140 mm) Darracq in November 1904.

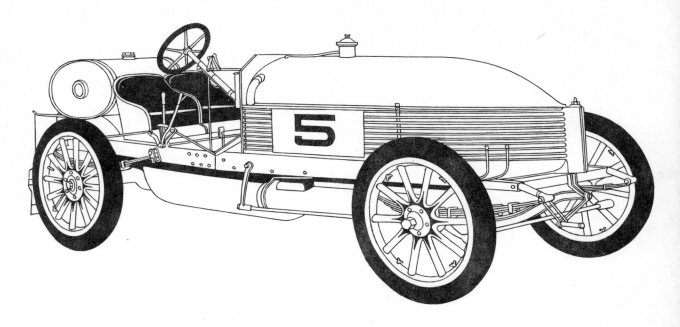

litre 4-cylinder car was somehow made to fit into the 1,000 kg. limit.

With a bore of 160 mm and stroke of 170 mm the engine was certainly large, but if the stated output of 70 h.p. is correct the specific efficiency was only about 5 h.p. per litre; however, it was remarkably light, with admirably designed aluminium crank case and other parts, with pistons and connecting rods drilled into the semblance of Gruyère cheese and with 1 mm thick sheet-copper water jackets soldered to the cylinder barrels. All this was a triumph of craftsmanship but a simpler solution, used by Napier and others soon afterwards, was to make thin copper water jackets by electrolytic deposition over wax cores which were melted away after a sufficient thickness of metal had been deposited.

Engines as large as this were necessarily slow running and atmospheric inlet valves still sufficient, but in order to improve breathing the Panhard Seventy had three small inlet ports and valves to each cylinder; these gave a greater port area, of course, than one large valve occupying the same space. In the next year, however, the old firm changed over to mechanical valves both for their racing and production models, and

NAPIER, 1905

The first English car to hold the record was the 6-cylinder (159 × 127 mm) Napier driven by Macdonald at 104.65 m.p.h. in January 1905.

the armoured wood chassis went into limbo at about the same time.

The ingenuity of the designer of the Seventy and similar monsters was equalled by the temerity of the men who drove them, but the writing was on the wall. In the Paris-Vienna Race of 1902 one of the light cars, Marcel Renault's 3-litre 16 h.p. Renault, was so much faster over the bad Austrian roads that all the advantage the big cars had gained on the good French roads was stolen.

The Renault's average speed over the whole racing distance of 615.4 miles was 38.9 m.p.h. whilst H. Farman's speed in his Seventy Panhard was fractionally less at 38.4 m.p.h. though the big car was probably 30 m.p.h. faster on a suitable road than the smaller. None the less the 'monster' racing car dominated the scene for some years, and the 1908 Grand Prix saw the first imposition of a capacity limit on heavy cars in a classic event. Therefore, in many ways, it was through the influence of Voiturette and Light Car racing that the advances were made which raised the average specific output of the touring car engine from about 4 h.p. per litre in 1900 to some 15 h.p. per litre in 1914.

We have seen how racing showed up the inadequacy of the Panhard-type of tiller steering and within a few years wheel steering was *de rigeur* even on those light cars for which some form of lever or tiller would have been perfectly suitable; the research into better materials for brakes was also stimulated by racing. Similarly the need for spring dampers (usually miscalled 'shock absorbers') was first made apparent on fast cars, and although Commandant Krebs of Panhard-Levassor patented a damper in 1899 the first recorded use of these devices was on the Mors in which Gabriel made such an impressive speed in the Paris-Madrid Race. Undoubtedly, however, the greatest boon the ordinary motorist received from the racing fraternity was the pneumatic tyre; it was, at the same time, his heaviest cross.

Reading between the lines it seems likely that the steam-carriage experimenters of the 1830's suffered breakdowns from the racking their vehicles had to accept from the pounding of steel-tyred wheels on rough surfaces. To stand the strains their vehicles had to be massively built, and the excessive weight, obviously, increased the stresses. These problems also confronted the motor car designers of the 'nineties.

Robert Thompson patented the pneumatic tyre in 1845 and used a

DARRACQ, 1905
A 200 h.p. Darracq, with V-eight engine (170 × 140 mm) raised the record to 109.65 m.p.h. in December 1905.

set on his own brougham, but his invention was ahead of its time and was forgotten. Thompson also built some heavy steam-tractor-cum-omnibus vehicles which, after experimental use in England, performed valiant service for some years in India, and for these he designed solid rubber tyres which were the first of their kind. These were quite satisfactory but rather short-lived and inordinately expensive, and it was not until the bicycle age that the rubber tyre really came into its own. The pneumatic tyre was re-invented by J. B. Dunlop in 1888.

The motor cars of the early 'nineties mostly ran on solid rubber tyres, which were satisfactory enough at speeds up to about 20 m.p.h. but not suitable for anything much faster. The solid tyre certainly could not puncture but it set up destructive hammering and vibration, and it could, and did, stretch and fly away from the rim in a variety of perverse and dangerous ways.

As far as can be ascertained the first motor car to be fitted with pneumatic tyres was a Peugeot which the Michelin brothers entered for the Paris-Bordeaux-Paris Race in 1895. The tyres were, of course, of Michelin's own make and similar to those being used at that time on some of the Paris cabs; they proved wholly inadequate at motor car speeds. They took twenty two spare inner tubes with them and used them all; when all the tubes were used innumerable punctures and bursts were patched by the roadside and the Michelin-Peugeot did not finish the course. Largely, one suspects, because M. Michelin and his crew were too exhausted by the labour of dismounting and re-fitting the tyres, and

STANLEY, 1906

The second and last time the record fell to a steam car was in January 1906 when Marriott drove this Stanley at 127.66 m.p.h.

one can see why Emile Levassor said at the end of the race that the pneumatic tyre would never be the slightest use for motor car work.

He was wrong; it would not have been possible for the motor car to develop as it did without the pneumatic tyre. Each year the tyres grew better, but each year cars became more powerful and faster and tyre design did not catch up with car design for a long time. In the first years of motor racing the higher speeds made possible by the pneumatic tyre were often nullified by the time spent in roadside repairs.

The 'beaded edge' high pressure tyre soon replaced the earliest type of bolted-through or built-on variety. It was easier to remove and replace but even so the labour was considerable: detachable and interchangeable wheels or rims did not materialise until surprisingly late, and each punctured or burst tyre had to be levered off its rim, with the wheel *in situ*, the damage repaired, or a spare tube inserted, the cover levered back and its security bolts — those damnable contrivances — tightened up without, the driver prayed, the tube being nipped and ruptured again. Then the tyre had to be inflated to anything between 40 and 100 lbs.sq.in. pressure with a hand or foot pump.

'BLITZEN' - BENZ, 1910
Barney Oldfield, the famous American driver, raised the record to 131.72 m.p.h. in March 1910 with this 200 h.p. 'Blitzen' Benz. (4-cyl. 185 mm × 200, 21.5 litres capacity).

All this was bad enough for the ordinary motorist, but for the racing driver and his mechanic, working against time, dealing with twenty, forty or even more flat tyres in the course of a single race was a truly herculean task.

The first attempt to ease this burden was the 'Stepney' spare rim which, complete with inflated tyre, could be clamped beside the rim carrying the deflated one. This was only a 'get you home' expedient and unsuited for high speed work. It was followed by different varieties of detachable and interchangeable rim and finally, in 1907, by the Rudge-Whitworth detachable wire wheel which fitted on a splined false hub by a centre-lock device. This presented the quickest means of dealing with a puncture, and the A.C.F. banned the Rudge-Whitworth wheel from the 1908 Grand Prix, apparently because none of the French manufacturers were using it and feared it would place them at a disadvantage. However, the centre-lock wheel soon became universal for racing cars, and was used on the best quality touring cars in England and Europe. It never achieved quite such popularity in the States, and some American cars were still fitted with fixed wooden spoked wheels with demountable rims at a surprisingly late date.

The frailty of the early pneumatic tyre presented the pioneer motorist with his greatest amount of trouble and expense; it was one of the factors which deterred many people from buying a car. Everybody expected tyre trouble — and got it. In the first years of this century a small, light car carefully driven at not more than 25 m.p.h. might travel 2,000 miles before the tyres were worn out, but anything over 1,000 was considered good and a journey of a hundred miles without a puncture was a rarity. For the heavy, fast car the trouble and expense were appalling: it is recorded, for example, that one rich young enthusiast unsuccessfully offered all the leading tyre companies £. 1,000 a year (of 1903 money) to keep his Rochet-Schneider racing car, converted for road use, equipped with tyres.

The American motor manufacturers seem to have inspired their tyre companies to good effect, and American tyres, particularly for light cars, seem to have been rather more reliable. There was a vogue in the U.S.A. for single-tube tyres, mostly made by Goodyear, which were a variant of Dunlop's original 'hosepipe' bicycle tyre. Though troublesome to

BENZ, 1914

By 1914 the land speed record regulations required the time to be based on the average speed of two runs taken in opposite directions. Therefore, Hornstead's speed of 124.1 m.p.h., though constituting the official record, was slower than the 1910 record in a similar Blitzen Benz.

repair these gave good service on the very light runabouts and steamers of c. 1900/01. In the winter of 1900 Hubert Egerton, the English agent, drove a Stanley-designed Locomobile steam car from Land's end to John o'Groats — that is, from end to end of the British Isles — and though he encountered every form of trouble, and reckoned to have consumed five tons of water, most of which had to be brought to the tanks in a little canvas bucket from wayside streams, he did not have a single puncture*. This was a truly remarkable record at that time, but the single tube tyres were only suitable for light and fairly slow cars and their popularity soon waned.

By 1914 the pneumatic tyre was still very troublesome and short-lived by present day standards, but it was so much better than it had been at first that the roadside struggles of the early days seemed like a nightmare. The influence of racing was almost wholly responsible for this improvement.

The fundamental basis of engine efficiency lies, obviously, in cramming the greatest possible amount of combustible mixture into each cylinder, burning it and exhausting it completely. In other words valves, valve ports, induction and exhaust passages, and combustion chamber forms are all of great importance. It was precisely in these departments that early engines were most lacking according to modern notions. The demands of racing stimulated designers, and although they were not generally considered suitable for ordinary engines before the 1914-18 war, overhead valve and camshaft arrangements of one kind and another were developed for sports-and racing-car engines from about 1906 onwards.

The need to improve 'breathing' became increasingly important when the unlimited engines of the 'monsters' gave way, under race regulations, to those of limited piston area, limited total capacity or limitation by fuel consumption as in the English Tourist Trophy contests and similar events. The piston area limitation of the 1908 Grand Prix still permitted engines of more than 12 litres capacity and the winner's average speed (Lautenschlager—Mercedes) was 69 m.p.h. In 1914, Lautenschlager again won but with a Mercedes of 4½ litres only, and on a more difficult circuit, but the average speed of the smaller car was only 4 m.p.h. less than that of its giant ancestor.

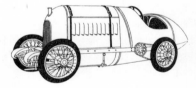

FIAT 300 GP, 1911
The 'monster' racing car was still in evidence in 1911 when this 300 h.p. Fiat lapped Brooklands at 154 m.p.h during a race. The engine capacity was no less than 28 litres.

* Doubt has been cast on this, as some reports say that Egerton had his wheels altered and fitted with ordinary beaded-edge Dunlop tyres.

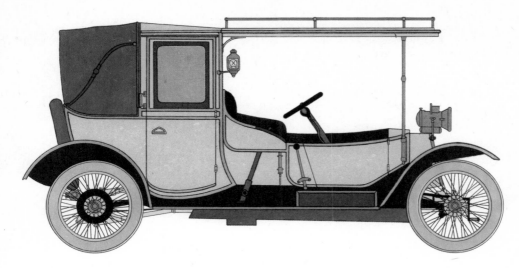

LANCHESTER 28, 1910

6-cylinder overhead valve engine, 42 h.p.
at 2,200 r.p.m. Swept vol. 223 cu.ins.
3-speed epicyclic gearbox with multi-disc
clutch for direct drive and oil-cooled
multi-disc brake. Lanchester worm-geared
live axle. Great Britain.

OPEL DOKTORWAGEN, 1909

4-cylinder 10/12 h.p. engine with variable
lift valves. Gearbox with 3 speeds forward
and reverse. Top speed about 35 m.p.h.
Darracq influence was still to be seen in
Opel design until 1910. Germany.

DAIMLER, 1910

4-cylinder Knight type sleeve valve engine, 38.2 h.p. Swept vol. 383 cu.ins. Rudge-Whitworth detachable wire wheels, and Lanchester worm geared live axle. Great Britain.

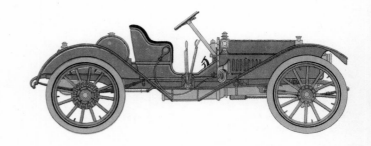

OLDSMOBILE, 1910

4-cylinder side-valve engine, 40 h.p. Swept vol. 277 cu.ins. Four speed gear box. Shaft and live axle. USA.

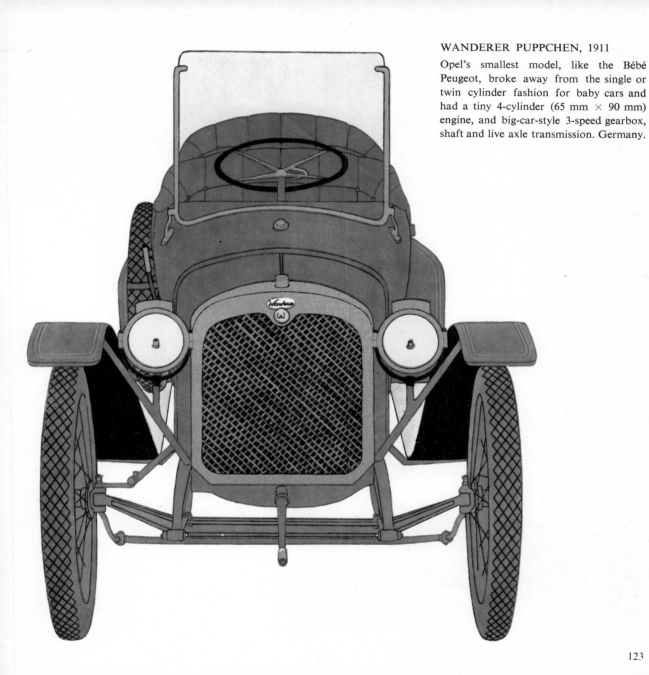

WANDERER PUPPCHEN, 1911

Opel's smallest model, like the Bébé Peugeot, broke away from the single or twin cylinder fashion for baby cars and had a tiny 4-cylinder (65 mm × 90 mm) engine, and big-car-style 3-speed gearbox, shaft and live axle transmission. Germany.

RENAULT 12/16, 1910

4-cylinder side valve engine, 15.8 h.p. Swept vol. 147 cu.ins. Cone clutch. Shaft and live axle. This particular car has an English drop-head "Doctor's Coupé"-body. France.

ADLER 12, 1911

4-cylinder side valve engine, 13.9 h.p. Swept vol. 111 cu.ins. multi-disc clutch. 3-speed gearbox, cardan shaft and live axle. About 35 m.p.h. Germany.

AUSTIN 7, 1911

1-cylinder water-cooled engine. Cone clutch and 3-speed gear box. (This car is really a Swift, built in the Austin works and given an Austin radiator). Great Britain.

DELAHAYE 10/12, 1912

4-cylinder side valve long stroke engine
(2,7" bore × 4.7" stroke). The "shooting-
brake" body is the predecessor of the
modern station waggon with room for
both passengers and cargo. France

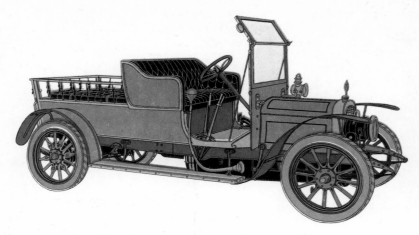

OAKLAND, 1912

4-cylinder engine, 45 h.p. Swept vol. 332
cu. ins. Popular winner in many hill climbing contests. USA.

MERCER 35, 1913

4-cylinder T-head side valve engine. 58
h.p. Swept vol. approx. 305 cu. ins. 4-speed
gearbox. Top speed about 75 m.p.h. The
Mercer "Raceabout" was one of America's most famous sporting cars. USA.

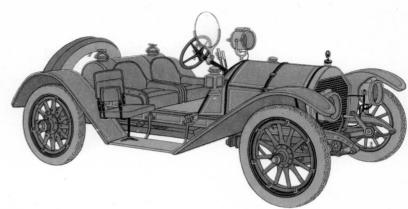

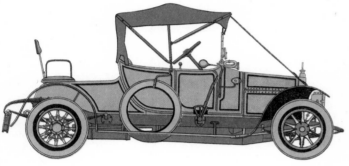

VERMOREL 12/16, 1912

4-cylinder side valve engine, 13.7 h.p.
Swept vol. 126 cu.ins. Top speed about
43 m.p.h. One of the many small engineering firms which went into motor car production before the 1914 war. France.

MORRIS OXFORD, 1913

4-cylinder T-head White and Poppé engine. 8-9 h.p. Swept vol. 62 cu.ins. 3-speed
gearbox, worm geared live axle. The first
of the famous "Bullnose" Morris cars.
Top speed about 50 m.p.h. Magneto ignition. Great Britain.

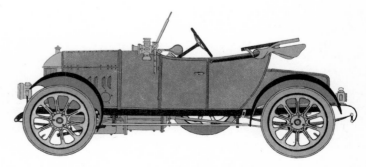

NAPIER, 1912

4-cylinder side valve engine. 15 h.p. Swept vol. 164 cu.ins. The first around-the-world trip by automobile was made by the American C.I. Glidden in a Napier, and Napier was the first manufacturer to make a commercially successful 6-cylinder car. Great Britain.

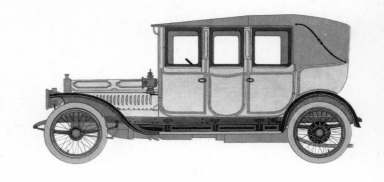

CHEVROLET, 1914

6-cylinder overhead valve engine, 24 h.p. Swept vol. 171 cu.ins. Weight about 2,225 lbs. Chevrolet became Ford's chief rival in the 1920's, with their cheaper 4-cylinder model. USA.

ARGYLL 15/30, 1914

4-cylinder single sleeve valve engine (Burt and McCullum patent). Swept vol. 160 cu.ins. Magneto ignition. Multi-disc plate clutch running in oil. Overhead worm drive. Four wheel brakes diagonally compensated. Scotland.

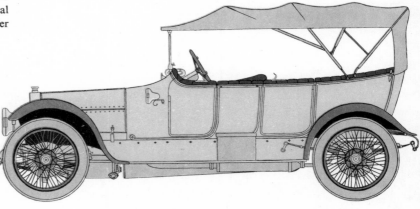

Many of the steps towards increased efficiency came, as we have seen, via the voiturette or light car classes. The former were dominated by single and twin cylinder cars until 1910 when, for the first time, a small 4-cylinder engine triumphed in the Coupe des Voiturettes. This was the Hispano-Suiza, designed by Marc Birkight, the cylinder dimensions of which were 65 mm bore x 200 mm stroke. This could run up to 2,300 r.p.m. and although not notably faster than the 'big single' Sizaire-Naudin of 100 x 250 mm, or the V-twin Peugeot of 80 x 280 mm the little Hispano had better acceleration and was less destructive of tyres.

The Hispano-Suiza engine was a T-head side valve, and the next significant step in the development of the small high-efficiency engine came with the single overhead camshaft and inclined valve arrangement, designed by Ernest Henry, for Peugeot, in 1911/12. This layout allowed good breathing, good combustion chamber shape and reduced the reciprocating weight of the valve motions. By 1914, engines built to this plan by the Sunbeam Company (whose Grand Prix car was based upon the Peugeot) developed a little more than 30 b.h.p. per litre and thus had more than five times the specific output of the best racing engines of 1900.

The expedient of supercharging was not much practised before 1914, though the possibility had been envisaged by Louis Renault as early as 1902. The first recorded supercharged engine was made in 1907 when Lee Chadwick of Pennsylvania used a single-stage centrifugal blower as a desperate measure to improve the very disappointing performance of his new 6-cylinder model, the porting and valve arrangements of which were so poor that the engine's output was less than that of the 4-cylinder Chadwick of similar cylinder dimensions. From this, it was but a step to using the supercharger, in conjunction with a re-designed engine, as a means of gaining success for Chadwick in competitive events.

As the magic figure of 60 m.p.h. was, for the first time exceeded (by a road vehicle, that is) by a Jeantaud electric car, Jenatzy's *La Jamais Contente*, in 1899, and as the Land Speed Record of 127.66 m.p.h. over the flying mile fell to a Stanley steam car in 1906, the fates of electricity and steam in speed events must be briefly mentioned.

The electrical excursion was, indeed, brief. Jenatzy and the Count de Chasseloup-Laubat, the two contenders for the record, realised that their freak electric cars were no more than freaks. After each brief timed

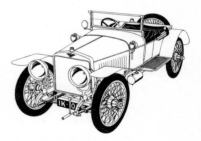

HISPANO-SUIZA, 1912
The 'Alfonso' Hispano-Suiza, was designed by Marc Birkigt and named in honour of King Alfonso XIII of Spain. It was as pleasant to drive as it was handsome to look at; capable of 70 m.p.h.

run over the flying kilometre their expensive batteries were not only exhausted but sulphated from too-violent discharging, and on more than one occasion motors were burnt out also in the U.S.A. In 1902 Baker made an attempt on the record in an electric car of remarkably advanced aerodynamic form, and exceeded 80 m.p.h. before the collapse of a wheel put paid to the experiment. This was the last serious attempt with an electric vehicle.

In passing, it should be mentioned that 100 m.p.h. was first 'cracked' in 1903 by Rigolly driving a 110 h.p. 4-cylinder opposed-piston Gobron-Brillié.

Steam fared better than electricity. The Count de Chasseloup-Laubat won the Marseilles-Nice-La Turbie Race of 149 miles in one of the De Dion Bouton steam brakes in 1897. His average speed was 19.2 m.p.h., and a similar brake, driven by de Dion himself, took first place in the class for four-seated cars in the relatively unimportant Paris-Dieppe event later in the same year. These were coke-fired vehicles which needed a 'chauffeur' as well as a driver, and the Marseilles-Nice-La Turbie affair was the only major event to be won by a steamer; also, soon after, de Dion and Bouton transferred all their energies to developing their petrol engines, but Léon Serpollet's more modern steam cars, with their 'flash' boilers and paraffin-burning automatic furnaces, kept the steam flag flying in hill climbs and some other events for a few years.

Although Serpollet steam cars (called Gardner-Serpollets after 1900), competed with distinction in long distance races until 1904, it was in hill-climbs and short sprint events that the particular virtue of the steam car, excellent acceleration, showed to great advantage. So much so that they were barred from many events which gave rise to the myths that the discrimination against them was unfair and that the steam car was 'killed by the opposition of the petrol companies'.

To dispose of the second myth first; all the later steam cars, among which the American Locomobiles, Whites and Stanleys, and the French Gardner-Serpollets (which were copied in Belgium and England) were particularly well known, burnt petrol or paraffin. As they burnt rather more than an internal-combustion car of comparable size and performance the petrol companies had no reason to oppose them. They faded from the scene ultimately because the petrol cars became easier

1912 Napier touring car: although
Napiers were responsible for the
first commercially successful 6-cyl-
inder cars (in 1904) they continued
to make 4-cylinder models like
the 15 h.p. type shown here.

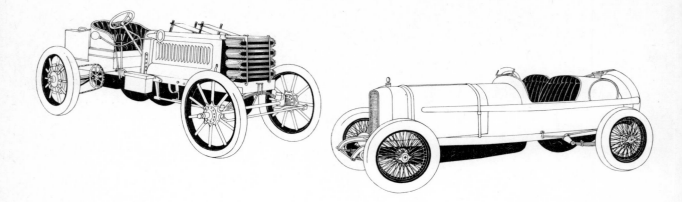

to handle and more reliable, whilst the best of steamers, though apparently simple, always needed more skilled care and maintenance than the average unskilled motorist can give.

As for the allegedly unfair discrimination, there appears, at first sight, to be an element of truth in this but it will not stand close examination. Most hill climb and sprint events were timed and handicapped on a rated horsepower basis: determining the horsepower of a petrol engine was difficult enough, but at least all could be judged on the same formula, but the output of a steam engine is directly variable with the pressure and even with a flash boiler, which only makes steam as required, it is possible to built up a reserve of heat in the tubes and so raise the horsepower developed far above the average output for a brief spurt. With a fire-tube pot boiler, such as the Stanley cars used, it was possible to build up a head of steam and raise the actual pressure considerably above normal. Therefore the organisers of events had some justification in thinking the business of finding a formula which would satisfy all parties was too difficult, and so took the easier course of banning the steamers.

The onslaught made upon the Land Speed Record by Fred Marriott driving a very special Stanley steam car at Daytona was the last great triumph for steam. As we have seen, the record was set by Marriott at 127.66 m.p.h. in 1906, and in the following year he tried again with a new car, 'The Rocket', which could work up to 1,300 lbs.sq.in. pres-

'SEVENTY PANHARD'

The famous 'Seventy Panhard' —a 13 litre 4-cylinder car built to conform to the 1,000 Kilos weight limit. (Top left)

SUNBEAM, 1914

The 1914 racing Sunbeam, with an overhead-camshaft engine based on the Henry-designed Peugeot, was faster than the 1902 'Seventy Panhard' though the engine was only a quarter the size.

sure. The actual speed he reached was not, alas, officially timed but was estimated to be not far short of 150 m.p.h. when the streamlined car hit a bumpy patch in the sand, flew into the air, landed at right angles to its course, rolled over and disintegrated in the most spectacular manner without, miraculously, killing the driver. The Stanley brothers decided, however, that they would take no further part in such enterprises.

In a book of this size it is not possible to do justice to the large subject of motor sport in all its aspects, but some mention must be made of such affairs as the Herkomer Trials, the Alpine Trials, and the Swedish Winter Trials which played an important part in proving the ability of cars to stand tough conditions. This particularly applies to the Swedish Trials, which helped manufacturers to open up new markets in Russia, and innumerable small, friendly but very tough Trials held in England.

Present day trials and rallies prove little but the depth of the purses of rival organizations, but the sporting contests of sixty years ago not only improved the breed but dispelled the public's belief that the motor car was no more than an ingenious toy for rich eccentrics.

PEAU DE BIQUE

The goat-skin coat as worn by the Chevalier René de Knyff and other pioneer motorists.

The bodywork of the earliest experimental motor cars was a mere afterthought, little more than a seat perched a-top the machinery, and when the car developed into an article of commerce, in the early 1890's, it was natural that the coachwork and fittings should follow established carriage patterns as closely as possible. Various mechanical details, however, obtruded themselves, and these dictated changes and finally demanded the evolution of quite new body styles which had little but their names — phaeton, cabriolet, victoria, dog-cart, brougham, land-aulet — in common with the carriages on which they were based.

The motor car designers at first had no option; they had to go to the established carriage builders. Similarly the carriage builders felt obliged, rather reluctantly at first, to provide the coachwork for the noisy stinking contraptions they so much despised. So we find very early in the business such famous names as Kellner, Rothschild, Mulliner and Hooper associated with the motor trade.

There were many difficulties. The established coachbuilders, like all craftsmen, were conservative, individualistic and hated working to rule, whilst the motor manufacturers soon saw that standardisation would be the key to prosperity in their new trade. They complained that coachbuilders would not work to drawing or pattern and that, in conse-

VAUXHALL 'PRINCE HENRY' 1912

The 'Prince Henry' type Vauxhall of 1912, had a side valve 4-cylinder engine of $4\frac{1}{2}$ litres capacity. Although other designers of high-performance cars were mostly adopting overhead valve and camshaft designs the Vauxhall showed what could be done with a conservative design if it was sufficiently well executed.

quence, time and money were lost in altering, drilling, cutting or filing before a body could be secured to its chassis. They also complained constantly (particularly with reference to closed bodies) that the coachbuilders *would* make everything too heavy. When a rated 12 h.p. engine really only developed 12 h.p. every ounce mattered. The coachbuilders, having their reputations at stake, disliked cutting down weight too much lest the work should rattle, fret and crack under the stress of motor car speeds. They complained in their turn that the short wheelbases, and high-pitched lines of the early chassis made it impossible to provide the elegant flowing lines and dignified spaciousness to which the 'carriage gentry' had become accustomed.

As long as only two seats were needed the body designer had a fairly easy task, and the 'Sociable' or 'Victoria' bodywork of the early Benz-type of car could be quite happily fitted in with the mechanical portions. Naturally enough though, the customer of the time thought a three horsepower engine would do the work of three horses (even the engineers themselves did not realise that for a short pull a horse can exert some 10 b.h.p.), and expected his car to carry himself, wife, two or three children, dog, possibly chauffeur or 'motor servant' and a quantity of baggage as well, and extra seats had to be provided.

Providing an additional forward-facing seat for two or three more passengers behind the driver's seat was not easy. The combination of short wheelbase, large diameter hind wheels and (usually) the presence of driving chains made access to the back seat very difficult. Double or 'Siamese' Phaeton bodies, as they were delightfully named, with two similar bench seats, one behind the other, *were* occasionally fitted to early cars of the Panhard or Daimler type, but in order to clear the hind wheels they had to be pitched ludicrously high.

An alternative solution was to have an extra seat, necessarily rather small, over the front axle, vis-á-vis fashion. This arrangement was only suitable for rear engined cars; it was popular on voiturettes of the De Dion Bouton type, and was occasionally found on the little Benz's. It was not too bad as an occasional seat for children but three or four adults crammed in a tiny voiturette found the vis-á-vis arrangement very cramping. Intelligent Reader will ask how the driver could see the road through the heads and bodies of his front seat passengers, to which

Motor-hat with face mask and mica window.

the answer is that he couldn't. Another solution, which at least allowed the driver to see where he was going, was to have dos-á-dos seats in dog cart fashion, or a wagonette type of body which allowed the rear passengers easy access to sideways-facing seats. This made for very cramped leg room and a sideways motion is not really comfortable for long journeys. The first satisfactory arrangement was the tonneau body which was introduced about 1897.

Tonneau, of course, means tub or cask, and the motor tonneau provided seating behind the driver's seat in an arrangement similar to the body of the 'tub' or 'governess' cart so popular with those who did not quite aspire to a carriage yet thought the trap or dog-cart a little too 'sporty'. With its door in the back and seats in the rear corners (plus an extra tip-up seat on the door itself usually) the tonneau could be made very comfortable; the passengers faced forwards, or nearly so, and had ample leg room. It was an essentially European and English style, and was less often seen in America; largely, no doubt, because by the time the motor car was really making headway in the States the tonneau body was going out of fashion. The name lingered on and old-fashioned people referred to the rear part of any car as the tonneau until quite recently.

The tonneau body's popularity lasted until about 1904/5, and it is

DARRACQ, 1899
Léon Bollée designed this 1899 Darracq, which has a horizontal air-cooled engine and 5-speed belt-and-pulley primary drive.

usually said that the inconvenience of stepping out through the back door into the muddy road caused its fall from favour. This was a consideration but the real reason was that the shape of the tonneau, and its rear door, made it difficult to arrange any weather protection.

At first the car was no more than a fine weather toy, but as it became more practical motorists naturally wanted windscreens and hoods so that they could use their cars in wet weather without having to dress like deep sea divers or get soaked to the skin. A few tonneau-bodied cars were supplied with detachable brougham heads — a sort of primitive 'hard top' — but these were not very convenient. Nor were the 'Lonsdale' hoods, adapted from the type of wagonette named after that famous sporting peer Lord Lonsdale, which were attached to each side of the car and met longitudinally in the middle when closed. More and more the demand grew for a 'side entrance' tonneau or rear compartment, and designers were obliged to provide longer chassis, mounted on smaller wheels, to meet the call.

The four- or five-seat open tourer, to which hood and windscreen could be added, thus came into being and was the commonest type of body to be fitted to large and medium sized cars for the next twenty years. The old rear-engined voiturette having now grown up into a scaleddown version of the big car with forward-mounted engine, became the two-seater (roadster in American usage), with a tool-box-cum-luggage platform behind the seat to which, as time went on, a folding 'dickey' or mother-in-law seat for occasional use was added.

Nearly all early cars appear to lack cohesion of design; the various parts bear little relation to one another. They may be interesting to look at and superb finish and detail work may make them impressive, but harmony of line and proportion were very seldom achieved. A notable exception is the first production model twin cylinder Lanchester of 1900/04 which was unconventional in almost every particular, but aesthetically satisfying as it was the first car to be designed as an entity and not as an assemblage of ill-assorted bits and pieces. It was also the first car which the occupants appeared to sit *in* rather than *on*. By virtue of its underslung worm-geared live axle, and cantilever suspension it had a longer wheelbase and lower floor level than its contemporaries which greatly enhanced its appearance.

ROLLS-ROYCE, 1910
Imposing limousine coachwork, probably by Barker, on a 1910 Silver Ghost Rolls-Royce chassis.

Dr. Lanchester saw that the car must be designed as a whole, and against his Directors' wishes he insisted that the Company made their own bodywork — an example which was only gradually followed. The result was as graceful as it was comfortable and efficient; but Lanchester was an exceptional man, combining mechanical genius with the eye of an artist. A similarly happy visual effect was achieved, in a different way, by Ransom E. Olds with that most famous early American 'gas-buggy' the little curved dash Oldsmobile.

The ordinary open touring car still rejoiced in high-sounding names like Park Phaeton, Clarence or Victoria but in the new century there was really very little link with the horse-drawn originals. A new name, the Roi des Belges, was introduced into coachbuilding circles and was used to distinguish an opulently curving, tulip-like form which, if executed really well on a big enough scale, could have a superb effect.

This type of body was also sometimes called the Tulip Phaeton but the more common name of Roi des Belges arose because one of the few un-amiable characteristics of that most unpleasing monarch, Leopold II, was his championship of the automobile. It is believed that the inspiration for the tulip-like curves came from the King's mistress, Cléo de Mérode. When she and His Majesty, together with a representative of Rothschild et Cie, the Paris coachbuilders, were discussing what type of bodywork should be fitted to the King's new Mercedes Mlle de Merode was moved to put two elegantly curved and buttoned easy chairs side by side and suggested that the seats and panelling of the new car should be similarly curved. There were those unkind enough to refer to the Roi des Belges type of body as the *Style Cleopold*.

The early touring cars gave the impression of a series of curves rising towards the back. The bonnet was generally low and was separated from the rest of the car by a vertical dashboard. From the foot of the dashboard the line curved gently to the riser of the front seat (front doors were rare before 1905 and if fitted were very low and followed the curve). Then a further series of curves carried the eye to the back rest of the seat which carried the curvature outwards. The line then flowed down again, and once more upward and outward to the highest point; this was the padded back of the rear seat which rose anything from six inches to a foot higher than the corresponding part of the front seat. If a wind-

MORRIS OXFORD, 1914
The ancestor of Britain's first mass-produced car— 1914 Morris Oxford with 4-cylinder, 12 h.p., White and Poppe engine.

screen was fitted it rose, to considerable height, from the dash-board.

From about 1906 onwards the line was gradually lowered and lengthened; the emphasis became more horizontal and the curves less voluptuous. For a given engine size wheelbases, generally, grew longer though much of the increase in apparent length was an optical illusion brought about by the straighter lines and greater coherence. A curved and upward sloping 'scuttle' (cowl in American usage) now extended back from the dashboard (which thus became the bulkhead or firewall), and the windscreen was moved back to the rear edge of the scuttle and consequently nearer to the passengers. Doors to the front seats became more common and finally universal. The seat backs still rose well above the upper limits of the doors and side panels, and the best coachbuilders still used curved surfaces and mouldings to good effect.

The final development of the open tourer before 1914 was the 'torpedo' or flush-sided body, in which the radiator was raised, the bonnet line tapered and also raised so that there was an almost unbroken sloping line from radiator to windscreen in place of the sharp change of radius at the scuttle. From the windscreen to the back of the car the line was again continued almost unbroken, the seat backs being flush with the body sides or very nearly so. In the hands of a sensitive designer, and done on a big enough scale, the 'torpedo' tourer could be most handsome. On a small scale it all too often resembled a bathtub on wheels.

Very early in the history of the automobile the fashion for an annual change took root, but on the whole the development of body styles was logical, though the whims of fashion could obtrude and some years saw a greater or lesser proportion of good shapes than others. There were, naturally, considerable differences between one firm and another, and national characteristics were also much more obvious than they are to-day. Early American cars give the impression of being more angular and stark than their European counterparts on the whole; also the 'sit' of the canvas hoods in the raised position was much more assertive. The typically German line, particularly from about 1910 onwards, betrayed a kind of Teutonic self assertion which gave a heavy and clumsy effect: this was very true of German closed cars. During this time it is difficult to choose between the best work of London and Paris, but some very fine coachwork was also executed in Belgium.

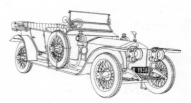

AN ENVIABLE POSSESSION

With its noiseless 7½ litre engine, and light open touring body the Silver Ghost Rolls-Royce could exceed 65 m.p.h or creep at walking pace in top gear.

Much of the beauty of a given body could be marred if the proportions of the mechanical parts were at fault. This is shown when the wheels of an old car are altered to take wide-section tyres. Some manufacturers always seemed to get the proportions just wrong; for example, the early six-cylinder Napiers had the radiators mounted just forward of the front axle and they always looked nose-heavy and lumpish. By contrast the contemporary Silver Ghost Rolls-Royces, the bonnets of which were just as long, had the radiators mounted just behind the axle and always looked right.

If the problem of designing an open motor car of seemly appearance was difficult, the task of making a closed body which did not look ungainly was almost insuperable, on account of the height. Even the best open cars of the period look much less attractive with their hoods erected.

With the large diameter wheels and other chassis and suspension characteristics of the time, the floor level of the average car was some two feet from the ground, and the expedient of saving height by having foot wells on either side of a transmission 'hump' would not have been acceptable. The sort of customer who could afford a closed car expected an unobstructed flat floor and plenty of leg room. The clothes and social customs of the period also dictated the need for really generous proportions from floor to roof.

The closed car was designed primarily as a formal carriage and as such it had to be suitable for formal occasions. Tall, silk-hatted gentlemen and their womenfolk, wearing those enormous confections of artificial flowers and furbelows which have been described as 'hats like well-kept graves', expected to be able to step up into their motor without stooping, to sit in relaxed but upright posture and still to have ample headroom for the most outrageous headgear the milliner could conceive. The result was that the distance from ground to roof might be greater than the wheelbase of the car, and the difficulty of achieving harmonious proportions in such a compass was formidable indeed. However, the better coachbuilders managed to achieve dignity and presence, even if grace eluded them. The modern notion of sliding into one's car folded like a jack-knife, and sitting crouched in a foetal posture would have horrified our grandparents.

Another trouble with the closed bodies was that they were very heavy

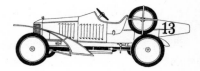

VAUXHALL, 1911

A 20 h.p. sporting model Vauxhall of 1911. This car had a 3-litre 4-cylinder engine and was driven by Hancock in the 1911 *Coupe de l'Auto* Race. This was originally an event for *voiturettes* but by 1911 was extended to *voitures légères*. This Vauxhall illustrates the state of development the sporting 'light car' had reached.

and set up considerable wind-resistance. Therefore, in the days when engine output only averaged around 5-8 h.p. per litre a chassis to carry closed coachwork, and still to have a reasonable performance on hills, had to have a very large and extravagant engine. Small-engined town cars and taxicabs were made, it is true, but these were not expected to have a maximum speed of much more than 25 m.p.h., and their progress in low gear up hills was tedious in the extreme.

The great size of the windows called for a great weight of heavy plate glass heavily framed, usually, in mahogany (the frameless window appeared just before the war); the sumptuous interior fittings, panelling, inlaid woodwork and upholstery also weighed a good deal, as did the lamps and external fittings, and the popular landaulet type of body called for very massive construction of the frame and supports for its folding leather 'head' if it were not to rattle and creak abominably.

So, not only did the coming of the motor car oblige the coachbuilding fraternity to design afresh it also revolutionised their methods. Most early motor bodies were panelled as well as framed with wood, and the steaming and shaping of $\frac{1}{4}$" thick mahogany panels to the flowing lines of a Roi des Belges body, for example, called for skill of a high order. To cut down both weight and cost metal panelling was adopted. Lanchester was one of the first manufacturers to make use of aluminium, not only for body panels and mudguards but for hinges, brackets and other body components. Aluminium panelling soon became established for the highest grade work, although difficulties were encountered at first in securing the rather ductile metal to wood framing. For lesser quality work sheet iron was used, and the old wooden panels were obsolescent by 1912. Present day manufacturers who boast of the rust proofing processes to which their steel bodies are subjected, and who then feel no shame when they crumble into holes after three years use, might learn much from the zinc or lead coating given to the sheet metal work of half a century ago.

The mudguards of the first motor cars were sketchy and inadequate; like those of carriages they were usually made of curved wood or glazed 'patent' leather stretched on an iron frame. It soon became apparent that motor cars needed wide generous mudguards, and flat sheet iron 'wings' with rolled mouldings, and the edges mechanically turned over suitable

BODYWORK

1. 2-seater, or roadster, with dickey seat, c. 1914. 2. Flush-sided 'torpedo' tourer, c. 1913. 3. Racing or sports car, re-bodied for road-use, c. 1910. 4. Coupé de Ville or Brougham, c. 1912. 5. Landaulet, c. 1908. 6. Landaulet fully opened canopy and windscreen removed, c. 1908. 7. Limousine, c. 1912. 8. Three-quarter landaulet with non-detachable roof opening at rear-quarter, c. 1910. 9. Touring car with detachable 'hard-top', c. 1910. 10. Fixed-head 'doctor's' coupé, c. 1914. 11. Owner-driver's saloon: rear doors only, access to front by gang-way between front-seats. c. 1914. 12. Enclosed-drive 7-seater Berline, c. 1911.

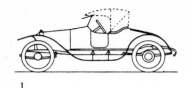

1

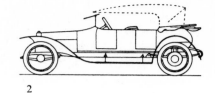

2

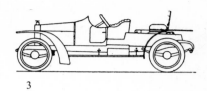

3

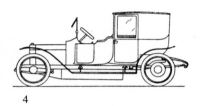

4

5

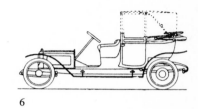

6

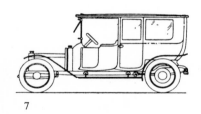

7

8

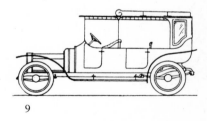

9

10

11

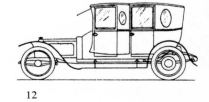

12

143

stiffening rods, came into use. They were often very attractively curved and flared. The domed mudguard, or crown fender as it was called in America, began to replace the flat variety from about 1912 onwards, and indirectly ushered in a new technique in body building.

This was the use of pressed steel sheet for panels (and ultimately frames) in place of the former hand beaten work. The craft of the 'panel basher' was not to die out for many a long year, indeed it is still very much alive, but the modern method of repetitive press-work for body building had begun on a small scale before 1914, and the domed mudguard was one of the first fruits. There are rival claimants to be first to make pressed steel bodies; the 1913 American Hupmobile is usually said to be the pioneer but it was probably antedated by a few months by the English B.S.A. concern.

For the most part, however, pre-1914 motor bodies were hand-made by traditional methods modernised but not fundamentally altered. More and more manufacturers set up their own body-shops and more and more use was made of jigs and special machine tools evolved for the job.

The painting, 'lining-out' and varnishing were also done in accordance with carriage-trade traditions; and when it is remembered that as many as forty coats of sealer, primer, undercoat, body-colour, finishing-colour and varnish, each allowed to dry for several days before being rubbed down and 'flatted' in readiness for the next might be used, it can be seen why a motor car might be ordered in early spring but not delivered until late autumn.

The beautiful gloss and depth of finish imparted by these methods were at once admirable and impractical. Impractical because the var-nished finish showed every mark and 'spotted' badly if put away wet. The painting processes had to be simplified, at least for the lower priced cars. Ford introduced a system of 'gravity painting' which was widely copied. The bodies were tilted on suitable cradles and the paint literally poured on, allowed to run down into troughs, and only a small amount of brush work was needed to get rid of ripples and waves. Drying ovens to speed the process were also used and tentative experiments with spray-painting were made.

In the first years of this century most manufacturers set a chassis price and the buyer than had to pay extra for the body of his choice (whether

DARRACQ, 1906
This 1906 Darracq 'Flying Fifteen' was one of the soundest medium priced cars of its time. It was relia-ble and capable of about 45 m.p.h.

supplied by the motor firm or by an 'outside' coachbuilder), the painting, the hood and windscreen (if fitted), lamps, tyres, tools and all the other essentials.

This makes it difficult to compare prices then and now, but it is fair to say that some of the accessories which we would regard as essential were very expensive. In 1910, for example, a good speedometer cost roughly the equivalent of £.100 in terms of 1966 values. Nearly all the fitments, lamps, horn, instruments, hub-caps, control levers, lubricators etc., were of brass and superbly made. The labour of keeping them polished was prodigious and as time went on the amount of brightwork diminished. Nickel or, occasionally, silver-plated fitments were beginning to replace brass by 1914.

The first motorists did their best to drive in the dark by the light of ordinary carriage candle-lamps, which were soon found to be totally inadequate. One of the troubles Emile Levassor suffered during his famous Paris-Bordeaux-Paris drive was the difficulty of keeping his candles alight as the vibration of the engine split the soldered seams of the lamps. Before the end of the century special oil-burning side and tail lamps had been developed and headlamps, to burn acetylene gas, were also available. With these, night driving was less hazardous but for many years most motorists avoided taking their cars out after dark as much as they could.

The acetylene headlamps grew larger, more complicated and costly as time went on. Elaborate arrangements of compound lenses and Mangin mirrors were used to focus the bat's wing flame of the gas burner. With all these aids the acetylene lamps gave a light which was reasonably adequate for the speeds of the period, and one which anti-motorists considered dangerously brilliant. The dazzle problem was recognised and some of the best lamps (notably those by Louis Bleriot who was in the motor accessory business before he took to aeroplane manufacture) had blue glass screens arranged to swing between burner and mirror at the pull of a lever and cable affair on the dashboard.

The oil-lamps were bad enough to keep clean in the days of dusty roads (and cleanliness was essential if they were to burn properly), but the acetylene ones were very troublesome. The gas generators, sometimes integral with the lamps but usually a separate apparatus carried on the

ROVER, 1907
A single-cylinder 8 h.p. Rover of 1907—one of the most popular light cars made in England.

running board, gave the motorist an unpleasant task after each use as the evil-smelling residue of spent carbide had to be emptied out, the filter cleaned and fresh carbide and water introduced. The American Autolite Company set up an excellent system, which allowed motorists to hand in an exausted cylinder of dissolved acetylene gas at almost any garage and, for a suitable fee, receive a fresh one in exchange. This did away with most of the lighting troubles, but no similar arrangement was set up in Europe or England.

As electric lighting for streets and houses had been in use since 1880 it may seem odd that motor cars still depended upon oil and acetylene gas for so long. The electrically driven cars — the American runabouts and those stately electric broughams and landaulets once so fashionable in towns for theatre- going and shopping — were fitted with electric lights naturally enough, and a few owners of petrol cars also fitted up electric lamps on their cars. But electric lighting really did not come in until the introduction of the tungsten filament bulb in about 1910, and another factor was that it was not until then that suitable small dynamos had been designed. The old-style carbon filament bulbs had been very inefficient in the small sizes suitable for vehicle lighting.

From the very earliest days various firms and individuals had experimented with small dynamos, to be driven from a car's engine or transmission shafting, so as to keep the ignition battery charged *en route*. The difficulty was to make a generator the output of which would not vary too widely at the different rates of speed, as the basis of early dynamo design was on the assumption that the speed would be constant. Once this hurdle was over electric dynamo lighting sets, sold as extras, began to be fitted to some of the more expensive cars.

Once the dynamo problem had been solved it was but a step to adding an electric starting-motor to the installation. The necessity for hand-cranking the petrol engine had always been one of its greatest drawbacks, and one which decided many would-be motorists not to buy a car. The business of 'winding up the engine', as it used to be called, was beyond the ability of most women; it was often exhausting and could be dangerous as 'backfires' could result in broken wrists, or worse. Many devices were patented and put on sale for starting car engines mechanically by means of levers and cables worked from the driver's seat, by giant

Dust coat and protective headgear worn by the smart automobilist in 1903

clockwork affairs, by compressed air (which worked well but was expensive to install) and in other ways which varied from the ingenious to the absurd. None of these 'self starters' was really satisfactory. As early as 1897 an Englishman called Dowsing had fitted his Arnold car (an English copy of the Benz) with an elaborate dynamotor which was supposed to keep a huge battery charged, to start the engine and to serve as auxiliary power on hills or in the event of breakdown; but nothing was done about electric starters on a commercial scale until much later. The Americans led the way.

The first car to be sold with full scale electric dynamo lighting and starting equipment, as standard fitments, was the Cadillac of 1912. The importance of fitting some reliable form of self-starter was impressed on Henry Leland, the head of Cadillac, when a close friend and associate, Bryan Carter (also a motor manufacturer), died as a result of gangrene after his jaw was broken when a starting handle kicked back and knocked him off his balance.

The components of the Cadillac electrical system were supplied by the Dayton Engineering Laboratories Company (Delco), who were already well known for their ignition coils, and this company also supplied the dynamotor and some other parts for the very elaborate 8/32 volt series-parallel starting and lighting system designed for the Lanchester cars of 1912 onwards.

The English and European electrical concerns soon followed the American lead: C.A.V., Lucas, Brolt, Bosch, Marelli and others were supplying starting and lighting sets before the 1914 war, but the motor manufacturers who made provision for fitting them invariably specified them as extras — and fairly expensive extras at that. The American manufacturers were much quicker to realise that the electric starter must be regarded as a necessity rather than a luxury, and by 1914 even a modestly priced car like the 18 h.p. Hupmobile was supplied with full electrical equipment at no extra cost. With the electric starter the last bugbear of the petrol car was beaten, and the last nail driven in the coffin of the steam car.

To describe all the other accessories, fitments and gadgets of the time, particularly the wonderfully elaborate and convoluted bulb horns, the exhaust whistles, gongs and other warning devices, would require a

This motoring dog does not look very happy—and who shall blame him?

book as large again as this one. The trade of motor accessory dealer naturally grew up with the motor industry and some very large fortunes were made. Then, as now, some pretty worthless 'gimmicks' were foisted on the public, but on the whole the accessories were useful (many, indeed, we would think essential, such as driving mirrors) and very well made. The social historian may propertly deplore the condition of the working class fifty or more years ago, but the plentiful supply of cheap skilled labour did mean that manufacturers did not have to skimp either the quality of material or the degree of 'finish'. One very curious aspect of the accessory trade is that that very simple and absolutely essential device, the automatic windscreen wiper, did not materialise until some ten years after the close of our period.

Much, too, could be written about motor clothing — the goat-skin coats, the leather jackets, breeches and gaiters, the chamois skin knickers 'for the lady automobilist', the ulsters and capes, the dust coats and veils, the goggles and gauntlets and all the other elaborate and voluminous garments with which our motoring forbears tried to fend off the chill and wet of bad weather or the nearly-intolerable dust of a dry day. As we look at the advertisements of the time we can only wonder at the fortitude of those who would appear in public in such uncouth habiliments, and at the social structure which made such elaborate garments, of such good materials, available at such relatively low prices: for nowhere was sweated labour more outrageously exploited than in the clothing trade.

Chapter 7

THE SOCIAL ACCEPTANCE OF THE MOTOR CAR

The 'Social Acceptance of the Motor Car' is an inadequate and some-what pretentious title for a subject so large that it can only be super-ficially touched upon as a conclusion to this book.

The transport revolution which the motor car initiated may one day be seen by historians as far more influential in shaping civilisation (whether for good or ill it is still too early to say) than some more tangible revo-lutions of the past. For who can deny that Henry Ford in his era was of greater significance in changing the American way of life, with similar repercussions in many other lands, than Abraham Lincoln or George Washington?

We have seen how it came about, largely fortuitously, that the motor car was 'invented' in Germany and nursed from feeble infancy to lusty childhood in France. The other two great industrial nations, England and America, contributed less in the first period; the one because (in large part at least) of restrictive legislation, and the other because of inadequate roads and a consequently slower growth of public demand.

It must not be supposed, however, that Great Britain was the only country to suffer from anti-motoring legislation; the only difference really was that in England the laws were passed before the automobile was born, whereas most other governments waited for the infant to

FORD T, 1915

A 1915 example of the famous Mod-el T Ford, fifteen million of which were built in nineteen years.

draw breath before attempting to smother it. The smothering process naturally varied from country to country, and it is significant that although no specific restrictions existed Carl Benz, to name but one of the pioneers, conducted most of his first experiments on the road under cover of darkness. The most liberal view was probably taken in France and the most repressive in Switzerland where, in some cantons, the motor car was prohibited altogether until the twentieth century was well advanced. In Eastern Europe, Turkey, Russia and further afield, also to a great extent in Scandinavia, the badness of the roads was sufficient to deter the would-be motorist until comparatively recently, and officialdom was concerned only with monetary restrictions.

In America the legislation varied from State to State, and some State's laws were, at first, almost as biassed as those of Switzerland or England, but on the whole America tolerated, accepted and finally catered for the horseless vehicle with greater alacrity and foresight than most other countries.

It is easy enough, in 1966, to sit in judgement upon our forbears and to deride their attitudes. The hostility shown to the motor car and its owner in so many ways, seems ludicrous in an age which has been taught to worship progress and change without reflecting that the progress may be backwards towards extinction, and that changes are not always for the better. Public opinion at the beginning of this century was much less attuned to change than it is now, and legislation is, after all, primarily a reflection of public opinion distorted by the built-in prejudices of politicians and tarnished by the insufferable superiority and bumbling incompetence which are the endemic diseases of Authority the world over. Therefore the laws necessarily passed to regulate the use of motor cars (and regulation was, of course, necessary) were all too apt to be over-cautious, unnecessarily complex (laws usually suffer from being drafted by lawyers) and, once established, too slowly altered to reflect changing conditions and opinions.

If England is taken as an example it is seen that once motoring was legalised by the 1896 Act local authorities, dominated by a horse-loving gentry, were less tolerant than the central authority. The Act set a maximum speed limit of 14 m.p.h. but gave the Local Government Board power to vary this downwards. The Board promptly influenced the

The Demon Motorist, as seen through the eyes of *Punch*.

various County, Borough, Urban and Rural District Councils throughout the country to reduce the speed limit to 12 m.p.h. with further reductions to 10, 8 or 6 m.p.h. in a number of towns and villages.

As time went on and motors became more common the working class attitude (for want of a better definition) changed from amused contempt of the automobilist to active dislike. This was not unreasonable as most of the first motorists were well-to-do, frequently contemptuous of those they considered their social inferiors and insensitive to them. Also the dust thrown up by the increasing number of cars from the untreated roads was a very serious nuisance. For the motorist it must be said that unlighted over-laden wagons, commanded by carters who were frequently drunk, sometimes asleep, occasionally both and invariably reluctant to budge from the crown of the road, and 'lady bicyclists' who were prone to fall off their machines at the sound of a motor engine, were amongst the many hazards they had to face.

The 'carriage folk', who not only occupied most of the magisterial benches before which motoring offences were usually tried, but were also predominant in parliament and the upper ranks of the administration, were unswervingly hostile almost to a man. The permissive legislation they subconsciously thought had been passed to appease a few eccentrics from their own ranks, and because of talk of some new industry being left in the hands of foreigners. But instead of just a hundred or so motor cars, to be used as playthings and soon forgotten, and a handful of vulgar manufacturers temporarily enriched, these damned horseless carriages were here to stay. Not only that, they were increasing alarmingly, they made a stink and a din, they raised the dust, the middle and even lower-middle classes were becoming motorists and thus clearly aping their betters—above all they frightened the horses and something must be done.

The objection that motor cars frightened their horses made one of the anti-motorists' most effective weapons, and one which was wielded to good effect on both sides of the Atlantic. The motor fraternity pointed out in vain that if left to himself, and given sympathetic handling, the horse was intelligent enough to come to terms with the motor car, as he had with the railway train; it was almost invariably the nervous and incompetent horseman whose animal shied and took fright. Few horse

Stranded by the wayside, or the joys of motoring. As seen by *Punch*.

lovers would look facts in the face: had they done so they should have welcomed the mechanical vehicle as the means of rescuing their favourite animals from cruel and degrading conditions. With the great increase in the size and population of towns the horse's lot in traffic was most damaging as the constant stopping and re-starting imposed great strain. There were few who cared to reflect, if indeed they realised, that the average working life of a London omnibus horse declined from seven years to three between 1845 and 1895.

By the Motor Car Act of 1903 every mechanical vehicle had to be registered with the appropriate local county authority (on payment of a fee in addition to the 'carriage tax' then levied), and fitted with large plates front and back to show the registration number. This wholly logical and necessary regulation infuriated most of our motoring forbears who waxed supremely indignant at being 'numbered like convicts and labelled like hackney carriages'. However, in return a grudging concession was granted, and the speed limit for private cars was raised to twenty miles an hour. The old 12 m.p.h. limit was seen to be unrealistic, but the coming of the slightly more liberal attitude coincided with an intensification of the hostility between motorists and the police and magistracy which left a legacy of bitterness which still persists.

One can detect subconscious motives. Many magistrates resented the slightly increased freedom given to the motorist by the extra 8 m.p.h., and determined to be tough in the matter of penalties. Sensing this the police saw an opportunity to get their own back on the 'nobs', the gentry, who, for the most part, treated the constable on his beat as a good fellow but very definitely an inferior fellow. Not unnaturally the police resented the 'here, my good man' attitude, but with very few exceptions the gentry were never 'in trouble with the police', as the lower orders were; but now the motor-owning gentry, at least, were delivered into their hands.

The era of the 'Police Trap' started, and became the chief topic in British motoring circles for some years. It was significant that traps were never set in awkward or dangerous places but on nice straight, safe stretches of country road where the motorist might be tempted (often unwittingly, no doubt, as speedometers were uncommon) into letting his speed creep over the magic figure of twenty. With methods of measuring

THE TERRIBLE CRIME

These be-furred and be-goggled automobilists have committed the terrible crime of exceeding 20 miles an hour—and the worse crime of being trapped. As seen by *Punch*.

the distance (usually a furlong) and timing the speed which varied from inefficient to incredible, with watches of dubious veracity, often with no stop mechanism and sometimes, even, with no second-hand, but with stout determination to book as many offenders as possible, two plain clothes constables would lurk behind hedges or trees, calculate the speed and then signal to a hidden uniformed man, stationed further down the road, who would then step out and halt the motorist.

In many areas, particularly in the south of England (the manufacturing districts further north were not so dominated by the landed gentry type of magistrate), the benches were so notoriously anti-motorcar that the local police soon realised their accusations would invariably be accepted no matter how dubious their methods of timing might be. The magistrates nearly always imposed the heaviest fines they were allowed to inflict, and generally accompanied their decisions with totally unwarranted gibes and insults. The administration of the law towards the motorist was brought into contempt which lingers yet.

The wider aspect of governmental reaction to the motor car must also be briefly considered. The attitude of most governments was, in essence, 'If we shut our eyes for long enough they might all go away — but while we must have 'em let's tax 'em.' Nobody can deny the justice of some form of motor tax to provide the means to maintain and improve roads, and to deal with the other social consequences of the transport revolution; equally nobody can deny the injustice with which many governments taxed both private and commercial vehicles very heavily, and then spent only a minute fraction of the revenue on the roads and ancillary services. During the period under review the American record is probably the best in this respect.

One factor which undoubtedly helped to allay dislike of the motor car was the royal approval which was bestowed upon it at a very early stage. King Edward VII, as Prince of Wales, bought his first motor car in 1898, and by the time he came to the throne in 1901 he was a confirmed motorist; he began to use the motor in preference to the horse-drawn carriage for certain official functions as well as for his private occasions. Queen Alexandra also took to the new mode with enthusiasm and even drove herself occasionally — though only, it is true, on the private roads of the Sandringham estate. Other royalties quickly followed suit.

'SPIRIT OF ECSTASY'
A famous mascot. Charles Sykes modelled the 'Spirit of Ecstasy' for Rolls-Royce.

As the most typical type of anti-motorist was also, very often, the type of person most prone to uncritical adulation of monarchy, the royal lead given in England and most European countries helped to break down prejudice. As we have seen, the King of the Belgians gave his name to a particular type of motor body, and other notable royal motorists included the Queen of Italy and Alfonso XIII of Spain, in whose honour one of the most famous of the Hispano-Suiza models was named the 'Alfonso'. Kaiser Wilhelm was not to be outdone by his uncle the King of England, whom he so much envied, and he too became a motorist early in the century together with Prince Henry of Prussia who instigated the Trials which bear his name. The Russian royal family also bought motor cars before the end of the nineteenth century (by a margin of weeks only), and many of the Indian princes and other Eastern potentates became motorists.

Royal approval helped things along but the one attribute of the automobile above all others which sold it to the general public, and gradually stilled the opposing voices, was its sheer utility. The motor car gave men and women a new freedom, almost a new dimension; and the difficulties, restrictions, taxes and the fulminations of the anti-motorists would not deter them. The concept of the motor car as a rich man's plaything has been over stressed, though this is understandable. In 1906 Woodrow Wilson, in his capacity as President of Princeton University, said that possession of a motor car was such an ostentatious display of wealth that it would stimulate socialism by inciting envy of the rich. The obvious fallacy of this pronouncement escaped him: the sight of a motor car was apt to incite the common man to own one if he could, rather than to change the social system.

It is obvious that the most famous names in motor manufacture at the beginning of this century were associated with large, powerful and very expensive cars which only the rich could afford. But for every Panhard-Levassor, Napier, Packard or Rolls-Royce were a score of single-cylinder De Dions, Swifts 'Merry Oldsmobiles' and similar cars which brought motoring to the middle class. Lower down the scale motor tricars, quads and other rather crude machines, of little luxury and less reliability, brought motoring of a sort almost down to the bicyclists' level. And there was always the second-hand market.

LANCHESTER, 1913

1913 38 h.p. 6-cylinder overhead valve Lanchester. By 1910 the Lanchester tiller had been replaced by a steering wheel, but until 1915 the other distinctive Lanchester features of the engine position, 3-speed epicyclic gearbox, worm drive and cantilever suspension were retained with detail improvements. The engine had horizontal overhead valves and developed 63 b.h.p. from 4.8 litres capacity: this was considerably above average for the period and gave the large luxurious car a top speed of 65 m.p.h.

The impetus which finally made the motor car a tool for living rather than a luxury came from the American manufacturers in general and Henry Ford in particular. The American reader who has persevered so far may well have concluded that the writer has been too condescending, or positively unjust, about the efforts of the first motor manufacturers in the United States. Though it may be hurtful to American pride it is true, in general, that American designers, like the British, lagged far behind France and Germany before 1900. Indeed, the only basic difference between the American and the English motor industry of that early period is that the English knew they were lagging and the Americans, broadly speaking, did not.

It should not be taken as a slur upon American inventiveness and enterprise to say that, in very general terms, their first motor designers occupied themselves in re-inventing the motor car, and that considered purely as an exercise in design, the *average* American car up to about 1905 was less technically advanced than its European counterpart. Having said this, it is only fair to add that there were many admirable native efforts in the American pipe-line well before that period and that a number of English and European motor cars of the time were just plain horrible both in design and execution. The particular genius of the American manufacturers lay less in designing motor cars than in designing and putting into effect rational methods of making them.

Several — perhaps a majority — of the engineers and business men who first took up the manufacture of motor cars were more concerned with cheap vehicles for ordinary folk than with the carriage trade. Carl Benz himself, as we have seen, visualised the motor car as an alternative to the pony and trap rather than to the barouche and pair, and De Dion et Bouton in France and Ransom E. Olds in America were two notable pioneers in quantity production: the production of the 'curved dash Oldsmobile' rose from 425 in 1901 to over 5,000 in 1904. This venture also represents an early example, but by no means the first, of the 'assembled' product for Olds made no attempt, as De Dion et Bouton did, to make all the parts in his own factory but bought engines from Leland and Faulconer and transmission units from the Dodge brothers.

The essential ingredient in reducing costs lay in increasing produc-

THE 'A-A'

An announcement by the Automobile Association which was formed in England in 1905 primarily to warn motorists of Police traps.

tion; whilst the motor car was made in dozens with a large amount of hand labour, however ill-paid, used in finishing and assembly, it could never be cheap. The road indicated by De Dion, Olds and others (and notably by Lanchester with his insistence on interchangeability of machined components) was followed with resounding success by Henry Ford. Ford has often been given credit for 'inventing' mass-production, but this is an over simplification. All the elements of mass-production had been appreciated, and to some extent practised in a variety of trades, for many years, but the Model T Ford was the first article to be made in sufficient quantity to warrant the use of the term.

Seen with hindsight it is clear that there was a large element of luck in the success of the Model T Ford, but although there is now ample evidence to show that Henry Ford was in some respects a somehat un-pleasant man, remarkable notably for ineradicable obstinacy, he should not be robbed of a particle of the credit which is undeniably due to him for his vision, and for the pertinacity with which he overcame all oppo-sition in order to make his vision palpable.

One sometimes suspects that the number of words written about the Model T equals the number of cars made during Tin Lizzie's nineteen years production life: the figure reached the formidable total of 15,007,033. It seems unnecessary therefore to enlarge upon the car's mechanical features, and it is only necessary to say that by the standards of the time (sales of Model T started in 1908) the Lizzie was well, if somewhat crudely, designed, very well made of excellent materials, with no waste of money on inessentials or unnecessary 'finish', and represented unsurpass-able value for money. It was also exceptionally easy to drive.

The Model T had its little weaknesses, most of which could have been eradicated quite easily. A little re-designing, for example, of the low-tension 'timer' in the ignition circuit might have overcome many of the starting difficulties which soon made the Lizzie a source of world-wide merriment, not unmixed with profanity from those who nursed a broken wrist or aching back after long and unrewarding toil at the starting-handle. Henry Ford stuck to his guns; apart from a few essential changes in some components, he would not accept modifications, for to do so would have undermined his concept of continuing the model, mechanically unchanged, for as long as possible so as to reduce the

THE GORDON BENNETT TROPHY

The trophy presented by James Gordon Bennett, the New York newspaper magnate, to be compet-ed for in the international races which bore his name.

unit cost, the selling price and spare-parts prices, whilst increasing the profit margin.

The man or woman who bought a Tin Lizzie therefore had to learn to love its little ways, and such was the car's 'personality' that its little foibles, its temperamental starting in cold weather, its habit of creeping forward and pinning the owner against his garage wall when the engine did fire, its tendency to petrol-starvation on steep gradients necessitating an attack in reverse gear, its liability to boil like a samovar on little provocation and its endemic weakness of rear engine bearers which led to cracked and leaking crankcases — all these little weaknesses were accepted as a small price to pay for a machine so tough and worthy.

The greatest virtue of the Model T was that it was the first car offered at so low a price with a really adequate power-to-weight ratio, and consequently a reasonable performance, excellent hill-climbing ability and the stamina to tackle really bad going. Hitherto the 'cheap' car, generally speaking, had been a one- or two-cylinder runabout with an engine developing about 8 or 9 horsepower and weighing, on average, about half a ton. Such a machine was pleasant enough on a good road, but with a full load would often be found unable to cope with a combination of soft muddy roads and steep gradients. Therefore it could not really replace the farmer's or small business-man's horse and buggy. With the Model T the Ford Company gave the 'man of modest means' a 'big car style' four-cylinder engine developing some 22 horsepower in a four-seater car weighing only about 14 cwt.

The measure of Henry Ford's success is seen not only in the fifteen million Lizzies made, but in the constant reduction in price. In 1908, 5,986 were sold and the price of the 4-seater was $ 850; by 1916 the number had risen to 577,036 and the price had fallen to $ 360. Making the necessary allowance for inflation this trend continued after the war.

All this was made possible by a great expansion of plants and factories in different countries, by continual revision and improvement of technical processes and above all by the introduction of the moving assembly line. This was the first manufacturing process on a big enough scale to warrant such a step. The effects reached far beyond the confines of Ford's own concerns, influenced all other motor manufacturers in time and stimulated the demand for better roads which had been growing in vol-

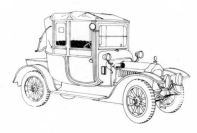

DOCTOR'S COUPÉ

Before 1912 almost the only type of enclosed car for the owner-driver was the coupé. It was particularly suited to doctors, hence the name. This example is mounted on a 1912 De Dion Bouton 12 h.p. chassis.

ume since the first appearance of the motor car. The most important aspect of the Model T was that it introduced a new concept into the relationship between producer and consumer which has had profound social consequences throughout the world. In *THE AMERICAN AUTO-MOBILE* John B. Rae says:

'Henry Ford was the first man not only to preach but to practice the doctrine that the buying public had a legitimate interest in the operations of a big business organisation, and he grasped a vital aspect of the relationship of mass consumption to mass production: namely that labour is something more than a commodity to be procured at the lowest possible cost. The worker is also a consumer. For this reason a distinguished French observer of American society, R. L. Bruckberger, insists in *THE IMAGE OF AMERICA* that for the twentieth century Ford's revolution is far more important then Lenin's. '

Because of the immense stimulus the Model T gave to the demand for 'cheap' cars, by acting as a sort of catalyst, the motor industry throughout America benefitted as did the trade in other countries in due course. Inevitably, however, this accelerated the collapse of hundreds of small companies whose products, very often, were technically inspired and of interest to the connoisseur.

Henry Ford was also regarded as a benefactor because he led the battle against monopoly, in the form of the attempt made by the Association of Licensed Automobile Manufacturers to regulate the motor industry throughout the United States by their control of the Selden Patent.

Space does not permit a full account of this fascinating subject, but, in brief, the Selden patent produced in America a situation similar to that which had existed in England when Lawson's syndicate attempted to monopolise the industry there through the purchase and re-sale of patent rights. George B. Selden, an astute attorney with a mechanical turn of mind and the gift of foresight, applied for a master patent for carriages propelled by internal combustion engines as early as 1877. As specified, the Selden vehicle would have been almost wholly useless, particularly as it was to be propelled by the Brayton type of 2-stroke gas engine which, at that time, weighed half a ton for a mere one horsepower output. Nevertheless the essential features of carburettor, clutch, change speed gearing and so forth were specified.

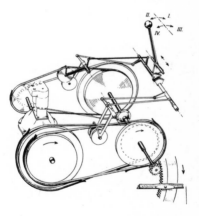

DAIMLER CONTROLS

Diagram of the mechanism and controls of the 4-speed belt-driven Cannstatt-Daimler carriages of 1894 onwards. The lever controlling the jockey-pulleys which tightened the belts worked in a similar fushion to the 'gate' or 'H-slot' gear shift.

By various means the grant of the final patent was delayed until 1896, when the time might have seemed right for exploitation. Selden has been accused of positively Machiavellian cunning in delaying his patent so long; if this is so, then he showed remarkable lack of fiendish calculation thereafter for it was not until 1899 that he sold his patent to a syndicate of Wall Street financiers, whose immediate objective was to put fleets of electric cabs on the streets of the principal cities. Quite why the promoters of an electrical automobile concern wanted a patent for an internal combustion vehicle' might not have seemed immediately apparent; but the business-men concerned were soon seen to be right to have other irons in their fire. Although some two thousand electric cabs were built, the 'Lead Cab Trust', as it was nicknamed, was as monumental a flop as a similar, but smaller, organisation set up in London in 1897/8; and when the business failed the Electric Vehicle Company turned its attention to making what it could of the Selden Patent.

The result was the formation of the A.L.A.M. in 1903, and a long series of court room battles arising from the Association's attempts to force all manufacturers to join their ranks, and to pay royalties on each car sold, under threat of prosecuting them and their customers in respect of each 'unlicensed' motor car sold. These tactics were exactly similar to those of the Lawson Syndicate a few years earlier, and the situation became positively Gilbertian. To quote again from John B. Rae *THE AMERICAN AUTOMOBILE*: — 'At this juncture the Ford Motor Company came into existence. Henry Ford did not believe in patents, but he enquired among friends in Detroit about the possibility of getting a license from the A.L.A.M. and was told that his application would be refused as he had still to demonstrate that he could build cars to the association's standards. What newcomers in the automobile industry were supposed to do is puzzling. They could not get a license "until they had established themselves as responsible manufacturers": on the other hand, if the Selden Patent was valid, no one could legally manufacture . . . without a license. The peak of absurdity was reached in 1908 when George B. Selden himself found the means to start making cars in Rochester and . . . was denied a license to manufacture under his own patent. As it happened, a year later he was able to become legitimatised by acquiring a defunct company that had a license, but the incident provided an illuminating commentary on the situation created by Selden's claims.

'At any rate Henry Ford and his business manager, James S. Couzens, decided to fight the patent. They were not alone... The battle raged in the advertising columns as well as the courtroom. A.L.A.M. members warned prospective purchasers, "Don't buy a lawsuit with your car", and Ford and his allies countered by posting a bond with each car sold guaranteeing the buyer against liability. Ford won both the legal and the public relations battles...'

Ford's decision to fight won him valuable public support, and although the business was not finally resolved until 1911 (when the patent had but a year more to run anyway), by a Court of Appeals ruling that it *was* valid but applied only to vehicles driven by Brayton-type engines. As the only such vehicles built were two constructed on Selden's behalf to demonstrate the practicability of his ideas (which they only did by the slenderest of margins), the whole long legal fight was really no more than a bout of shadow boxing, but the affair firmly established Henry Ford as a folk hero — the little man pitted against monopolistic 'big business'. The irony of the situation was that by 1911 Ford was the biggest man in the business; but he did pass on the benefits of mass-production to his customers in the shape of lower prices, and to his work people in the form of above-average wages.

Motor car enthusiasts in England, and writers on motor car matters, have long been unjust about the average American car of the years immediately before the Great War. If one leaves out of account those American manufacturers who still concentrated upon making small numbers of splendid cars regardless of cost (the names of Mercer, Chadwick, Lozier, Pierce and others spring to mind), it is fair to say that the *average* run-of-the-mill Yankee car had less about it to attract the connoisseur than its European or British counterpart.

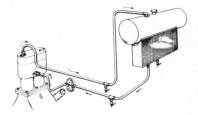

HONEYCOMB

An early example of the 'honeycomb' type of radiator forming part of the cooling system of the Canstatt-Daimler belt driven cars of c. 1897.

Where the engine of the typical European car would bedazzle the eye with its 'snailed' aluminium crankcase and burnished copper or brass pipes and fitments, the typical American engine seemed a dull affair of rough cast iron. This was thought 'cheap and nasty' on this side of the Atlantic, but the attention to unseen details of design, and the progress in iron founding in the U.S. really meant that, within its limits, the American engine was cheap and good. Good, that is, in the sense of reliable, durable and smooth running. Output for a given unit of capacity was usually rather less than that of a comparable European engine (and this has made another stick to beat the American designer with), but in a land where petrol was cheap and taxation by rated horsepower, or cubic capacity, was unknown, there was no point in trying to extract the last ounce of power from a given size. The large and relatively inefficient engines could be made agreeably 'unfussy' to drive behind, and because they were not highly stressed simple splash lubrication systems were adequate and helped to keep costs down.

To the European or English eye the American car of the period often seems unduly low geared, and not very good in the braking department. Here again, the manufacturers were merely being logical. They were not making cars for enthusiasts and they realised that the majority of their customers were not in the least interested in 'performance', hated changing gear and therefore were quite content to sacrifice a bit of acceleration, or maximum speed, in exchange for top-gear flexibility. They realised, also, that their customers did not want to spend their leisure time polishing a lot of brass (which was expensive anyway), and neither knew nor wanted to know the difference between understeer and oversteer. Therefore it was a waste of time and money to build into their cars the sort of road-holding, steering and braking qualities demanded by the *cognoscenti* in England and Europe.

The difference in attitude between European and American manufacturers is comparable with the difference between the finest English watch of the last century and the Waterbury — the first 'cheap' watch to be mass-produced in the U.S. The Waterbury concern chose a form of escapement, the Duplex, which was regarded as obsolete in England; no money was spent on jewelled pivot-holes and there was no meticulous finish and polishing of pinions or pivots to reduce friction; the work was quite roughly finished but the machines which made the parts were highly ingenious, and finally the Waterbury watch was furnished with so powerful a mainspring that, like the Model T Ford, it had no option but to go or bust. And as the design was much more clever than the casual glance might detect, go it did to remarkably good effect.

The watch collector will naturally prefer the 'Best London made', keyless fusee, free-sprung, English lever watch with minute-repeating work, jewelled in every hole and cased in 18 carat gold, but nobody can deny that Waterbury earns its honoured place in horological history by bringing a watch within reach of the poor man.

So it was with the mass-produced American motor car. The work which was begun in the Old World in the late nineteenth century was brought to its logical conclusion in the New World before 1915. Germany may claim to be the birthplace of the modern motor car, France its nursery, England the country where it learnt good manners, but nobody can deny that it was in America that the little fellow was taught his real place in the world.

This charming 'automobiliste', rather insecurely perched upon a somewhat improbable horseless carriage, beckons the Parisians of 1895 to a Motor Show.

1860 - 1910

FIFTY YEARS OF PROGRESS

1860   The first commercially successful internal-combustion engine
patented and put on the market
by Etienne Lenoir.   Page 21

1862   Lenoir adapts his gas-engine to
burn liquid fuel and experiments
with it in a road vehicle. Page 21

1865   Act of Parliament passed in England restricting 'Road Locomotives' to 4 m.p.h. in the country,
2 m.p.h. in towns, and requir-
ing a man to walk ahead carrying a red warning flag. Page 19

1872   Gottlieb Daimler, working for
Otto and Langen, begins experimental work on the 4-stroke
engine.   Page 21

1873/5 Siegfried Markus experiments
with internal-combustion engined
carriages in Vienna. Page 22

1876   Patent granted, and manufacture started, for Daimler's 4-
stroke engine under the name of
the 'Otto Silent Gas Engine'.
Page 21

1882   With Wihelm Maybach as assistant, Daimler sets up his own
experimental workshop. Page 28

1884/5 Carl Benz builds an experimental 3-wheeled car driven by 4-
stroke engine of $^3/_4$ h.p. Page 22

1885   Daimler granted patent for light
'high-speed' petrol engine; uses
one to drive wooden framed bicycle.   Page 29

1886   Daimler fits 1½ h.p. engine to
converted carriage for demonstration purposes.   Page 29

1887/8 Benz builds improved 3-wheeled
cars, grants French agency and
manufacturing rights to Emile
Roger. Benz cars begin to be
sold to the public. Page 25-26

1888   Léon Serpollet patents instantaneous steam generator (the
'flash' boiler) for use in light
steam carriages.   Page 30

1889   Messrs Panhard et Levassor
granted French manufacturing
rights in the Daimler patents,
and start manufacture of Daimler-type engines.   Page 30

1890   Daimler Motoren Gesellschaft
established in November, to develop, produce and sell Daimler
engines and horseless carriages.
Page 56

1891   Emile Levassor designs the first
petrol engined car combining
a forward-mounted engine, foot
controlled clutch and sliding
pinion change-speed mechanism. This year also saw, probably, the first experimental Amer-
rican petrol car—the Lambert.
Page 32-58

1892   Benz enlarges his motor car business and begins serious pro-

duction with a new four wheeled
model.   Page 26

1893   Frederick Simms granted licence to use the Daimler patents
in England.

1894   The first properly organised contest for self-propelled vehicles—
the Paris-Rouen Trial—is held.
A De Dion Bouton steamer is
first to finish the course, but the
event is not a race and first
prize is divided between Panhard
et Levassor and Peugeot, both
of whom use Daimler engines.
Page 37

1895   The Duryea Motor Wagon Co.
formed—the first American business expressly founded to build
petrol-engined motor cars. Frederick and George Lanchester
make a trial run in the first full
scale 4-wheeled petrol car of
wholly British design. Emile Levassor drives single-handed to
cover 732 miles in 48$^3/_4$ hours,
from Paris to Bordeaux and
back, in the world's first officially organised motor race.
Page 58, 60, 36

1896   Henry Ford constructs his first
experimental motor quadricycle.
A Panhard-Levassor car wins
Paris-Marseilles-Paris, 1062 ½
miles, at average speed of 15.7
m.p.h. The Locomotives on
Highways Act removes some of
the restrictions on motoring in
Britain and raises speed limit
to 12 m.p.h.   Page 57, 60

1897 The Comte de Chasseloup-Laubat wins Paris-Marseilles-La Turbie in a De Dion Bouton steam 'brake'—the only classic road race to be won by steam. Page 130

1897 Alexander Winton drives a car of his own design from Cleveland to New York, 707 miles in 78 hours, 45 minutes.

1898 An 8 h.p. Panhard-Levassor, with the new four cylinder engine and wheel-steering, wins Paris - Amsterdam - Paris, 889 miles, at average of 26.9 m.p.h. Page 109

1899 Sixty miles an hour exceeded by a road vehicle for the first time— on April 29th. by Jenatzy, over a flying kilometre, driving his cigar-shaped electric car '*La Jamais Contente*'. Page 38, 130

1900 The success of the 1,000 Miles Trial organised by the Automobile Club of Great Britain and Ireland gives a great fillip to the motor industry in Britain. The Chevalier Rene de Knyff averages 43.8 m.p.h. for 209½ miles in Circuit de Sud Ouest; the car, a 16. h.p. Panhard-Levassor. Pages 64

1901 Quantity production begins. De Dion Bouton sell 1,500 of their little rear engined voiturettes in year ended April 1901. Ransom E. Olds builds 425 'Merry Oldsmobiles' in his first full year of production. Page 156

1903 The Motor Car Act raises the speed limit in Britain to 20 m.p.h. Fatalities in the Paris-Madrid Race bring Town-to-Town racing to an end. Spyker exhibit a 6-cylinder car. Page 152, 112, 96

1904 One hundred miles an hour exceeded. Rigolly. driving 110 h.p. opposed-piston Gobron-Brillié timed at 103.56 m.p.h. over the flying kilometre. Page 112

1906 The last triumph of steam. Frederick Marriott, driving a Stanley, at Ormond Beach, timed at 127.66 m.p.h. over the flying mile. The Rolls-Royce 'Silver Ghost' model appears. Page 132

1907 In trying to beat his own record Marriott reaches a speed, untimed, said to be nearly 190 m.p.h., but the car overturns and disintegrates, the attempt is naturally abandoned and no more steam cars attempt to beat the Land Speed Record. Page 133 A Rolls-Royce Silver Ghost is driven 15,000 miles on test, with Royal Automobile Club observers aboard. 14,371 miles are without involuntary stoppage and at the end of the trial the car is dismantled; the cost of replacing those parts which show any trace of wear amounts to only £.2-2-7.

1908 After much wrangling F. R. Thomas declared the winner of New York to Paris Race. The car, is a 6 cylinder, 72 h.p. 'Thomas Flyer'. Of greater significance is the fact that the first Model T Fords are on sale by October. Page 157

1910 The Land Speed Record is raised to 131.72 m.p.h. by an American, Barney Oldfield, driving a German car-200 h.p. 4-cylinder 'Blitzen' Benz. Page 118

VEHICLES ILLUSTRATED

ACKNOWLEDGEMENTS

The author and publishers acknow-
ledge with many thanks the permission granted by Messrs. Hugh
Evelyn & Co., and their artist
George Oliver, for permission to
reproduce the following pictures
which were originally drawn for
their book Veteran Cars: Page 122,
1910 Daimler, Page 124, 1910 Renault, Page 127, 1912 Vermorel and
1913 Morris Oxford, Page 128,
1914 Argyll.

The following organisations and
individuals are also warmly thanked
for the help they have given or the
photographic material they have
lent:

Francis Hutton-Stott, Esq.
The Technical Museum, Stockholm.
The Science Museum, London.
The Montagu Motor Museum,
Beaulieu, Hampshire.
The Veteran Car Club of Great
Britain.
The Long Island Automotive
Museum, U.S.A.
The Smithsonian Institution, Wash-
ington DC, U.S.A.
The Ford Motor Company, Dear-
born, Mich., U.S.A.
General Motors, Inc. Detroit,
U.S.A.
Goodrich, Inc. Akron, U.S.A.
The Renault Organisation, France.
S.A. Peugeot, France.
Rolls-Royce Ltd., London.
Adlerwerke, Germany.
Daimler-Benz AG, Germany.
Adam Opel AG, Germany.

Museo dell'Automobile, Monza,
Italy.
Museo dell'Automobile, Torino,
Italy.
Museo Tecnico Leonardo da Vinci,
Milan, Italy.

First published in Great Britain in
1967 by George Allen & Unwin

Designed and produced by
A B Nordbok, Sweden

This edition published in 1984 by
Treasure Press
59 Grosvenor Street
London W1

© 1967 Tre Tryckare, Cagner & Co,
Gothenburg, Sweden

ISBN 0 907812 78 3

Printed in Czechoslovakia
50 545